A day in the life of

THE
AFRICAN KITCHEN

a safari chef, by Josie Stow and Jan Baldwin

INTERLINK BOOKS

An imprint of Interlink Publishing Group, Inc.
New York • Northampton

4

First American paperback edition
published 2005 by
INTERLINK BOOKS
An imprint of Interlink Publishing
Group Inc., 46 Crosby Street,
Northampton, MA 01060
www.interlinkbooks.com

Commissioning Editors:
Suzannah Gough and Stuart Cooper
Editorial Cookery Consultant:
Jenni Muir
Creative Director:
Leslie Harrington
Art Editor:
Lawrence Morton
Production Controller:
Oliver Jeffreys

ISBN 1-56656-580-4

Colour origination by Sang Choy
International, Singapore.
Printed and bound in China.

RIGHT: Watermelon, Mint and Vodka Sorbet (page 130)
ABOVE: Marinated Venison Kebabs (page 115)

Hello, I'm Josie.

My love affair with Africa and life in the bush began back in 1992 when I accepted an offer to cook on a horseback safari in South Africa. For a young English girl from Suffolk this was a daunting task: the camp had no electricity and most of the cooking was done over an open wood fire or on a two-plate gas burner.

I was soon having to deal with all kinds of exciting situations: buffalo in the camp, snakes in my larder and rhino grazing outside my tent at night. My supplies had to be fetched from 90 miles away in a four-wheel drive vehicle. Despite this, I became fascinated by the African culture, especially the cooking techniques and ingredients. My assistant Anna could speak no English, but we soon became friends and she began to show me the wonderful food culture that lay waiting to be discovered. It was here that I met my husband, Fred, who was a ranger at the camp. Our relationship started with cooking lessons; I couldn't understand why it was taking him so long to master a simple quiche until it was too late.

Since then, Fred and I have worked on a number of game reserves and lodges. In Kwa-Zulu Natal, I worked for Phinda Forest Lodge and found the local people incredibly resourceful, growing their own corn, beans, pumpkins and Zulu truffles. Utilizing my time off to visit the chefs' homes and gardens, a two-way process evolved. While I was teaching African people to cook in a professional kitchen, I was learning about their food culture and soon realized what wonderful culinary talent lay dormant among these delightful people. However I was amazed that most lodges and restaurants were serving European-style food. "South African" food consisted primarily of butternut soup and Cape Brandy tart — it was too westernized.

From Phinda I went on to develop the kitchens at Makalali in the Northern Province, near the Kruger National Park. My great friend Lori-Ann Newman came over for a short visit and I convinced her to stay and help me. Lori has a natural flair for cooking and loves to experiment with food and flavors. In retrospect, I don't know if I could have coped without her. It was while working together at Makalali that many of these recipes were created and we would often discuss new dishes under the shade of an old lemon tree.

As we began exposing the guests to African food, we broke every convention we could think of, even the traditional breakfast, and what we couldn't find in the local culture we borrowed from the rest of Africa. Our philosophy was simple: an unpretentious food style that was true

to itself and its surroundings, full of bold flavors, colors and textures. We were having the time of our lives, experimenting with abandon, unhampered by rules or conventions. The kitchen came alive. We encouraged our staff to taste, discuss, to sing and celebrate their own culture. It was a journey of discovery that altered our views on food forever.

We felt it was important that the chefs interact with the guests, and take pride in growing, cooking, and presenting their own produce. In the kitchen we had a map of the world on which the chefs would locate the guests' countries of origin. Lori and I would introduce new ingredients and explain where they are produced and how they are used — the one that most fascinated them was saffron, because it is more expensive than gold. It was very rewarding when the chefs were able to announce their menus to the guests and could impart their knowledge of the ingredients — soon they were cooking with enthusiasm and flair.

Food is precious in Africa. It is also a labor of love, whether you are sowing seeds, rearing livestock, gathering wood to fuel the fire, or pumping water and carrying it back home. Food is more than sustenance, it is a time for sharing. Meals are communal and eaten with the hands. By touching the food, feeling it, eating becomes a delightfully relaxing and intimate activity.

African cooking has always been wonderfully sociable. In most traditional African villages you can still see the women sitting under a tree, shelling nuts or singing, chanting and chatting as they rhythmically pound corn with a large, hand-carved pestle and mortar, called le hudu and le mose. It is a place for laughter and gossip, for building the close family bonds that are the envy of other cultures. Recipes are traditionally passed down from generation to generation by word of mouth and never rely on exact quantities. A handful, a calabash (a hollowed gourd) or a mug are the usual forms of measurement and cooks rely on feel, taste and memory.

Utensils are crude: for example, the stones for cracking nuts are used for generations, their shapes evolving through continual wear. In Africa many contented hours are spent choosing appropriate stones, weaving beautiful baskets, making sturdy clay pots, and carving and decorating gourds. Seasonal fresh produce like chilis, beans, mealies and pumpkins are dried, often on the roofs of homes or specially built huts, so that they can be stored and used in cooking throughout the year. Even in the heat and bustle of the safari lodge kitchen, the emphasis has always been on sharing and having fun, and I have a great deal of respect for this joyous, idyllic approach to food and cooking.

Braais or barbecues are synonymous with life on safari. The tradition stems from the days of early explorers, hunters, and pioneers. For me, it evokes images of a crystal-clear winter sky, jackals calling in the distance, a flickering fire and the aroma of sizzling meat and wood smoke. In the bushveld areas, the best coals come from hard woods like the camel thorn and lead wood trees — lead wood cannot be cut with a saw, only a hammer can shatter it. These woods produce coals that often stay hot enough overnight to prepare breakfast on the next morning.

Braaing is an art and it may take you a few attempts to become adept. For success you will need a wire brush, basting brush, long-handled tongs, a fire poker, a spade and a good source of light. Charcoal can be used instead of wood.

To start the fire, place a ball of dry grass in a circle of stones on a cleared patch of ground. Add some small twigs, then large logs and light with a match. A gentle blow will soon fan any smoldering grass into flame. For a wood fire, you will need to allow 1-1½ hours for the coals to burn down. Be sure not to start cooking too early over coals that are too hot. You need very hot coals to braai thinly sliced meat that requires quick cooking: at this high heat you should barely be able to hold your hand 2 inches above the grate for 1 or 2 seconds. For medium-hot coals, you should just be able to hold your hand over the fire for 4 to 5 seconds — this is the heat that most of the red meat in this book is cooked on. For a medium fire to cook white meats and fish you should be able to count 6 to 8 seconds. To cook food buried in the coals, or to keep food warm, a very low heat is required; the coals should ideally be turning to ash and you should be able to count 8 to 10 seconds. The heat can be adjusted by scraping the coals together or spreading them apart with a shovel, or by raising or lowering the grate.

Heat the grate over the fire's first flames and then scrub it clean with a wire brush to remove the remains of the previous braai. Before you start to cook, make sure you have everything you need and that the accompanying dishes are ready. Meat should be taken out of the fridge well in advance and brought to room temperature.

Most of the braai recipes in this book can be cooked under a broiler in a domestic oven. Preheat the broiler to the temperature required and rub off any surplus marinade from the food. Broil, turning from time to time and basting with the marinade until cooked.

Ingredients are often hard to obtain in Africa and you must be flexible in your requirements. Even placing a simple order can be an ordeal. I remember having to stand on the hood of a Land Rover to get a signal on my cell phone to speak to the supplier. There was a time when the delivery truck was unable to cross the river because of floods and all my ingredients had to be carried across the river by hand. Often the wrong items would be sent and suppliers would run out of ordinary things like tomatoes or lettuce. It taught me to be patient, resourceful, and very flexible.

These frustrations prompted my chefs and me to start our own garden, or shamba, which can be a hazardous undertaking on a game reserve with hungry hippos and baboons. We gave a neighbor a bottle of whisky for the use of his tractor and harrow and soon the garden took shape. It had to have an electric fence to frighten off hungry midnight raiders, but somehow the monkeys could always sense when the current was off. Chefs were often seen running out of the kitchen crashing pan lids together to keep the intruders away.

We all agreed the garden had to be organic so we started a compost heap and developed our own organic controls, such as garlic and soap solutions to spray around the plants to keep bugs at bay. Soon we were reaping wonderful crops of beans, carrots, chilis, and lettuces. It was always a relief to go into the garden and celebrate our first harvest of the year. Guests would come for a guided tour of the shamba and it became a focal point of the lodge.

Basic ingredients

African spinach or morogo

These terms refer to the leaves of many edible plants and may include the leaves of silver beet, sweet potato, pumpkin or edible wild plants such as buffalo-thorn. Choose the young and tender leaves and peel the stalks if they seem tough. This is done by breaking off the stalk and pulling the outer strands down the stem as you would de-string runner beans.

Buttermilk

The low-fat milk left over from making butter, buttermilk has a slightly sour taste. In Africa, it is used in baking and in marinades to tenderize meat.

Chilis

Chilis are a popular ingredient in African cooking and the climate is well suited to growing them. Some Africans chew the whole pod as the perspiration it causes cools the body in the intense heat of summer. Rich in vitamins A and C, chilis vary greatly in strength and variety; much of the potency is in the seeds and veins. They can be quite addictive once you have developed a tolerance for the heat.

Mealies or corn

Mealie is the African word for maize. Mealies are grown in carefully tended fields and, to facilitate wind pollination, they are planted in rows. The work is predominately performed by women. After harvesting, the mealies are eaten fresh or dried, husked and ground to mealie meal. There are several varieties, including white and yellow mealies. The kernels are chunkier than sweet corn and not as sweet, however sweet corn is an appropriate substitute for mealies in the recipes in this book.

Mealie meal

This is maize that has been dried and finely ground into a meal. It is usually cooked to give porridges of different consistencies. The staple dish of Africans and one that accompanies every meal, it is called sadza, ugali, bogobe or mealiepap depending on the region. When cooked to accompany stews it is rolled into a ball with the hands and dipped into a sauce.

Peanuts or groundnuts

Peanuts are sometimes called groundnuts because the seeds (or nuts) ripen underground. When the plant is ready to produce the seeds, the flower stalk bends down into the soil and a pod containing one or two seeds develops. The plant is very versatile. When harvested, the leafy tops are fed to

TOP ROW FROM LEFT Buttermilk, fresh chilis, dried chilis, sweet potatoes, peanuts
BOTTOM ROW FROM LEFT Josie unpacks supplies, pineapples, pumpkin leaves, mealies

cattle as they are very high in protein. The nuts are eaten as a snack or used in cooking. They can also be crushed to produce peanut oil, which is used in cooking or as lamp fuel.

Pineapples

This sweet fruit is grown extensively in the sub-tropics. Once picked, pineapples will not continue to ripen. Test them for ripeness by smelling the base for a fragrant aroma and pulling out one of the central spikes — it should come away easily if the pineapple is ready to eat. Imfulafula (home-brewed pineapple beer) has become a South African tradition.

Plantains and bananas

Plantains are similar to bananas and, when unavailable, green (unripened) bananas can be substituted. Plantains cannot be eaten raw because they are bitter and unpalatable. In Africa, bananas are used in both sweet and savory dishes. They are high in carbohydrates and, when unripe, primarily contain starch that turns into sugar as the fruit ripens. The leaves are used for wrapping food before cooking.

Pumpkins and squashes

There are endless varieties of squashes: acorn squash, gem squash, butternut, pumpkin and Hubbard, to name a few. The flat white Boer pumpkin is a typical South African variety. Pumpkins grow well in arid countries. They can be kept for several months and are often seen stored on the roofs of African houses. The nutty seeds are rich in oil and are used in cooking as well as roasted and eaten as snacks.

Spices

Africa produces vast amounts of spices, which have played an important role in the continent's culture and trading history. It is best to buy whole spices and grind them yourself as needed. A mortar and pestle can be used, or a coffee mill kept just for spices. Toasting spices before use intensifies their flavor and aroma. Always store spices sealed in airtight containers in a cool place away from direct sunlight.

Sweet potatoes

In Africa, sweet potato dishes are made to celebrate everything from births and marriages to deaths. The different kinds vary in color and are used in both sweet and savory dishes. Sweet potatoes are very high in fiber and are said to provide relief from digestive disorders.

Basic recipes

Preserved lemons

Ingredients
Lemons
Coarse sea salt
4-6 bay leaves
10 black peppercorns

Special equipment
Canning jar

Method
1 Sterilize the canning jar.
2 Determine the number of lemons that will fit into the jar and then weigh the lemons to establish how much salt is required — you will need about ½ cup of salt per 2¼ lb of lemons.
3 Wash the lemons thoroughly.
4 Cut the lemons into quarters from the top to the bottom without slicing them right through to the ends.
5 Carefully open out the lemons and sprinkle some salt into the flesh.
6 Place in the jar, sprinkling salt in between the lemons and adding the peppercorns and bay leaves as they are packed into the jar.
7 Add enough freshly squeezed lemon juice to cover the lemons, leaving a little gap at the top of the jar.
8 Seal the jar, then shake it thoroughly, turn it upside down and leave it to stand overnight.
9 Shake and turn the jar once a day for the next 30 days.
10 When the skins are soft and ready to use, remove a piece of lemon from the brine, wash it thoroughly in cold running water, discard the pulp and use the rind as required.

Preserved lemons are typical of Morocco and are used to flavor tagines and sauces. They need to be made a month in advance and can be kept for up to a year. The number of lemons required for this recipe is the number that will fit into your canning jar, plus a few extra to give you the lemon juice.

Harissa

Makes 1 cup

Ingredients
8 chilis
4 cloves garlic, crushed
1 tsp salt
2 tsp caraway seeds
1 tsp coriander seeds
1 tsp cumin seeds
A large bunch of mint, chopped
½ cup olive oil

Special equipment
Spice grinder

Method
1 Chop the chilis, garlic and salt together to form a paste.
2 Transfer them to a bowl.
3 Grind the spices together.
4 Add the spices to the chili mixture with the chopped mint.
5 Whisk in the olive oil.
6 Pour into a jar or bottle, seal and refrigerate until needed — leave for a day if possible to allow the flavor and heat to develop.

Harissa is a fiery hot spice condiment used in North African cuisine. If you love chilis you will be hooked on this! It will keep as long as the mixture is covered in oil and refrigerated.

Niter kebbeh

Makes 2 cups

Ingredients
9 sticks butter
1 onion, chopped
3 cloves garlic, crushed
¾ in fresh ginger, grated
1 stick cinnamon,
  about 1½in long
2 whole cloves
⅛ tsp freshly grated nutmeg

Special equipment
Cheesecloth
Sieve

Method
1 Slowly melt the butter in a saucepan.
2 Carefully bring it to the boil and simmer until the solids (white foam) have come to the surface.
3 Add the remaining ingredients and simmer slowly for about 50 minutes or until all the solids have fallen to the bottom.
4 Dampen the cheesecloth, fold it in half, and use it to line the sieve.
5 Rest the sieve over a bowl and strain the butter mixture through it.
6 Repeat the straining process a couple of times, then discard the solids.
7 Transfer to a screw-top jar and allow the niter kebbeh to cool before sealing.

Niter kebbeh is a spiced clarified butter used in the making of Ethiopian stews such as Doro Wat. It will keep for 1 to 2 months and can also be frozen.

Ras el hanout

Makes about ½ cup
Ingredients
4 bay leaves
1 tbsp ground cinnamon
1 tbsp coriander seeds
1 tbsp cumin seeds
1 tbsp ground ginger
1 tbsp black peppercorns
1 tbsp dried thyme
1 tsp cayenne pepper
1 tsp ground nutmeg
½ tsp aniseed
½ tsp cardamon seeds
½ tsp whole cloves
½ tsp mixed spice

Special equipment
Spice mill

Method
1 Place all the ingredients in a spice mill and grind them to a powder, then store the mixture in a sealed container.

Moroccan shopkeepers are renowned for their spice blends. Ras el hanout literally translated means "head of the shop." It can be a blend of 20 or more spices and some say it has aphrodisiac qualities.

Mint chutney

Serves 8

Ingredients
½ cup raw unskinned peanuts
3 cloves garlic
1 chili
½ cup fresh mint leaves
2 tsp coriander seeds
1 tbsp sugar
Juice of 1-2 limes
1 cup plain yogurt (optional)
Salt and pepper

Special equipment
Le selo or clean kitchen towel
Food processor

Method
1 Preheat the oven to 350°F and roast the peanuts until the skins are lightly toasted and beginning to crack.
2 Remove the skins — if you have a le selo, tip in the roasted peanuts and rub them around with your hands until the husks come off; alternatively, place in a kitchen towel, bundle up into a ball and roll the ball around on your hand to remove the husks.
3 Tip the nuts into a colander and sift out the husks.
4 Set the peanuts aside to cool.
5 Chop the garlic and chilis together to make a paste and transfer the mixture to the food processor.
6 Add the mint, coriander seeds and sugar and process the mixture until it is coarsely combined.
7 Add the lime juice to taste, then mix in the yogurt by hand, if using.
8 Season the chutney to taste then place it in a bowl, cover and store in the refrigerator until needed.

An African version of traditional mint sauce, this hot piquant mixture is delicious served with lamb. Adding yogurt makes it smoother and milder.

Berbere

Makes 1¼ cups

Ingredients
1 tsp ground ginger
½ tsp ground cardamon
½ tsp ground coriander
½ tsp fenugreek seeds
¼ tsp freshly grated nutmeg
A pinch of ground cloves
1 onion, chopped
2 cloves garlic
3 tbsp red wine
2¼ cups paprika
2 tbsp cayenne pepper
½ tsp ground black pepper
About ½ cup sunflower oil
Salt

Special equipment
Food processor
1 sterilized jar with lid

Method
1 In a dry frying pan, toast the ginger, cardamon, ground coriander, fenugreek seeds, nutmeg, and ground cloves over a low heat until they are fragrant, then set aside to cool.
2 Place the toasted spices in a food processor with the chopped onion, garlic and ½ tablespoon of salt and process, adding the wine slowly to form a paste.
3 In a saucepan, toast the paprika, cayenne, black pepper, and 1½ tablespoons of salt, stirring constantly, until fragrant.
4 Remove the paprika mixture from the heat, add the onion spice mixture and gradually stir in 1⅓ cups of water.
5 Place over a low heat and cook, stirring constantly, for 10 to 15 minutes.
6 Transfer the mixture to a sterilized jar, pressing down to remove any air pockets, and allow to cool.
7 Cover the spice paste with the oil, put the lid on and store in the fridge.

This is an Ethiopian red pepper spice paste used in dishes such as stews and Kifto (see page 104). It will keep for about 6 months.

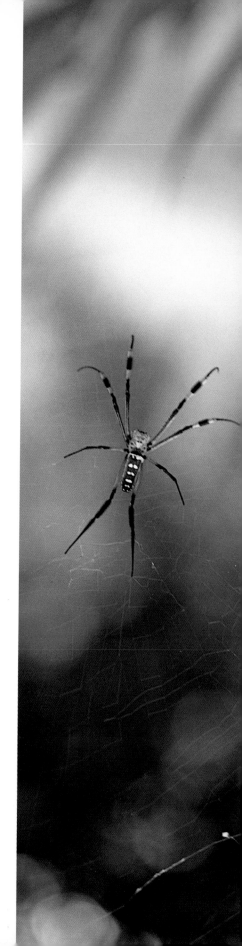

Biltong

Makes 3lb 6oz

Ingredients
3¼ cups white wine vinegar
About 8 lbs beef, sliced ¾in thick
and no wider than 3in

For the spice mixture:
¼ cup salt
¼ cup ground coriander
¼ cup cracked black pepper
¼ cup brown sugar

Special equipment
Large plastic container
Several metal hooks
Drying rack
An electric fan or other means of
   ensuring constant air circulation

Method
1 Mix together the vinegar and 3¼ cups of water.
2 Lay some strips of meat in a large plastic container in a single layer and shake over a little of the vinegar solution.
3 Combine the ingredients for the spice mixture in a bowl and sprinkle some over the meat.
4 Add another layer of meat and repeat the process until all of the ingredients are used.
5 Cover with plastic wrap and refrigerate for 6 hours, turning the meat over after 3 hours of curing.
6 Hook the meat strips at one end and hang them on the rack, ensuring the pieces of meat do not touch.
7 Leave the biltong to dry for 3 to 4 days in a continuous flow of warm air, then slice and eat.

Biltong was devised as a way of preserving game or beef before refrigeration. Colin Baber owns The Vaalwater Slaghuis (butchery) in the Northern Transvaal, South Africa and is renowned for his biltong. He uses quality cuts of meat from Bonsmara cattle reared on his bushveld farm. Bonsmara are a breed indigenous to South Africa and are esteemed for their tender meat. Colin says the animal must be fat — which generally means a cow of 4 to 7 years — and the freshly butchered meat must be hung for 1 to 2 days before preparation. To make biltong, you need a dry area (free from flies!) where warm air can easily circulate around the meat. Colin hangs his up in the butchery near the fans of his fridges and freezers.

Wake-up, rise and shine

As the dawn's first rays streak upward on the eastern horizon, you hear the patter of footsteps outside your tent. "Ko-Ko," comes a faint call. A beaming face appears at the tent flap, balancing on her head a tray holding a thermos of steaming coffee, some fresh fruit and a plate of rusks. You hear the muchinda (waiter) filling up the shower bucket while a dawn chorus twitters in the trees above. Drowsily, you head into the open-air shower to quickly freshen up. Over the screen of rough timber poles, you spy a few elephants enjoying an early morning drink at the watering hole. Muffled by the cool morning mist, a bushbuck barks further up the valley. Excitement grows at the thought of another safari in the African bush.

Behind the scenes, the lodge is coming to life. Fires are being lit and water is boiled. Rangers and trackers warm up their Land Rovers, before preparing hot boxes of muffins, tea and coffee, and cool boxes with cold drinks. Rifles are loaded and checked, the game drive routes discussed. Back in the kitchen, the chefs are lighting the gas ovens. The day's menu is written up on a board ready for the early morning shift to start work. Equipment and food are ticked off the checklist before being loaded onto waiting vehicles for the surprise bush breakfast.

Slipping into your comfortable khakis, you grab a hat, binoculars and camera and head for the open Land Rover where your ranger awaits. Everyone clambers aboard. Your tracker sits on the hood, eyes flitting left and right, looking for signs of last night's activity. The ranger thinks that a pride of lions made a kill in the early hours of the morning. Tension mounts as the vehicle bounces over the rough track. The tracker signals and the ranger slows down. They confer. A pride of five lions crossed the road last night, heading east! They shouldn't be far off, the ranger explains: the lions killed last night, and it's getting hot, so they will soon lie up.

Suddenly, the tracker points. Nervously, you scan the bush line and there, under the sickle bush, are two huge lionesses and three cubs. The ranger carefully inches forward. The lions lazily observe your approach while you frantically click away.

Driving away from the sighting, you sigh in relief and suddenly feel hungry. After a while, as if reading your thoughts, the ranger stops and, within seconds, he has laid a cloth on the hood with tea and coffee. Rummaging around in the green canvas hot box, the tracker offers around a tin of delicious, freshly baked muffins, their centers filled with apricot jam....

"Tummy crisis" dried apricot and muesli muffins

Makes 12

Ingredients

For the topping:
½ cup brown sugar
2 tbsp toasted muesli
2 tbsp butter
2 tbsp flour
½ tsp ground cinnamon

For the muffins:
¾ cup dried apricots, finely chopped
1 cup fresh orange juice
1 tbsp orange zest
1 cup buttermilk
9 tbsp butter, melted
½ cup honey
2 eggs, lightly beaten
1¾ cup wholewheat flour or nutty wheat flour
1¼ cup self-rising flour
1¼ cup toasted muesli
¼ cup wheatgerm
2½ tsp baking powder

For the filling:
4 tbsp apricot jam

Special equipment
12-hole muffin pan, greased

Method

1 Preheat the oven to 350°F.
2 Mix all the topping ingredients together in a small bowl and set aside.
3 To make the muffin mixture, combine the chopped apricots, orange juice and zest and allow to stand for 10 minutes.
4 Stir in the buttermilk, melted butter, honey, and eggs.
5 Combine the flours, muesli, wheatgerm and baking powder in a large bowl and make a well in the center.
6 Add the apricot mixture and stir with a wooden spoon just until the mixture has combined — be careful not to over-mix.
7 Spoon half the mixture into the greased muffin pan, until they are half full.
8 With the back of a teaspoon, make a well in the center of each muffin and then fill with a teaspoon of apricot jam.
9 Spoon the remaining muffin mixture on top, gently pressing it down around the apricot jam to enclose it.
10 Sprinkle the tops of the muffins with the muesli topping.
11 Bake for 20 minutes.
12 Cool slightly before removing from the pan.
13 Carefully ease a teaspoon around the edge of each muffin to loosen it, then transfer to a wire rack to cool completely.

These are excellent to take on early morning game drive to eat with a cup of coffee when your tummy is starting to think of breakfast!

Rusks

Makes 36

Ingredients
9 cups self-rising flour
4 tsp baking powder
2 tsp salt
2¼ sticks margarine, chopped
3 cups light brown sugar
2 cups sunflower seeds
3 cups All-Bran cereal, crushed
A handful of raisins
1 tbsp aniseed
2¼ cups buttermilk
½ cup sunflower oil
2 eggs, beaten

Special equipment
Shallow baking dishes

Method
1 Heat the oven to 350°F.
2 Mix together the self-rising flour, baking powder, salt and margarine until the mixture resembles fine breadcrumbs.
3 Add the sugar, sunflower seeds, crushed bran, raisins and aniseed.
4 In a bowl, mix together the buttermilk, sunflower oil and eggs.
5 Add the milk mixture to the flour mixture and stir to form a dough.
6 Use your hands to shape the dough into 36 balls and place them closely together in two rows on each baking dish.
7 Bake for 1 hour or until a skewer inserted in the dough comes out clean and the base sounds hollow when tapped.
8 Remove from the dishes and set aside to cool on a wire rack.
10 Separate the rusks and leave them to dry out completely in a very low oven set to 250°F.
11 Allow the dried rusks to cool before storing them in an airtight container.

Rusks are a dry biscuit traditionally eaten by South Africans and dunked in their early morning tea or coffee. They were introduced by the Dutch as a long-lasting alternative to bread on trek. Some of our guests thought they were stale cookies and threw them away, only to be horrified when presented with them again the next morning. Only after they complained did we realize we had to explain what they were. A ranger's mother gave me this recipe.

Chocolate chip cookies

Makes 20

Ingredients
9 tbsp butter
½ cup dark brown sugar
⅔ cup superfine sugar
1 egg, beaten
½ tbsp milk
1 tsp vanilla extract
1¼ cups flour
½ tsp baking soda
½ tsp baking powder
7oz dark chocolate,
  chopped
1 cup rolled oats
½ cup pecans, coarsely
  chopped

Special equipment
Baking sheet, greased

Method
1 Preheat the oven to 350°F.
2 Cream the butter and sugars together until light and creamy.
3 Beat in the egg, milk and vanilla extract.
4 Sift together the flour, baking soda and baking powder.
5 Fold the flour mixture into the butter and egg mixture.
6 Fold in the chopped chocolate, oats and pecans.
7 Cover the mixture and refrigerate for about 1 hour.
8 Roll the mixture into balls the size of a walnut and place them on the baking sheet, spaced well apart.
9 Gently flatten the balls into ½ inch thick cookies.
10 Bake for 8 to 10 minutes.
11 Cool the cookies slightly on the baking sheet before transferring them to a wire rack to cool completely.

This cookie mixture can be made in advance, stored in the refrigerator and baked when required.

Coconut and lime cookies

Makes 24

Ingredients
7 tbsp butter
½ cup white sugar
½ cup flaked coconut
1 tsp freshly squeezed lime juice
1 tsp finely grated lime zest
1 egg, beaten
1½ cups plain flour
1 tsp cream of tartar
½ tsp baking soda
¼ tsp salt

Special equipment
Baking sheet, greased

Method
1 Cream the butter and sugar together until light and fluffy.
2 Add the flaked coconut, lime juice and zest and mix well.
3 Beat in the egg.
4 Sift together the flour, cream of tartar, baking soda and salt and fold them into the butter mixture until a dough forms.
5 Place the dough on a sheet of wax paper and roll into a cylinder about 2 inches in diameter, twisting the ends of the paper together.
6 Place in the freezer until the dough is firm.
7 Preheat the oven to 400°F.
8 Peel the wax paper away from the cylinder and cut the dough into ¼inch round slices.
9 Place the cookies on a greased baking sheet and bake for 5 to 7 minutes.
10 Remove from the oven and cool on a wire rack.

Peanut butter cookies

Makes 24

Ingredients
1¼ sticks butter
½ cup superfine sugar
⅔ cup light brown sugar
1 egg, beaten
½ cup crunchy peanut butter
½ tsp vanilla extract
1⅔ cup plain flour
1 tsp baking powder
½ tsp salt
2 egg whites
**1¼ cup peanuts, unsalted and
  finely chopped**

Special equipment
Baking sheet

Method
1 Preheat the oven 350°F.
2 Cream the butter and the sugars together until pale and creamy.
3 Beat in the egg, then the peanut butter and vanilla extract.
4 Sift the flour, baking powder and salt together.
5 Fold the flour into the butter and egg mixture until smooth — be careful not to over-mix or the dough will become oily.
6 With your hands, roll the mixture into small balls.
7 Lightly whisk the egg whites with a fork to loosen them.
8 Roll the balls in the egg whites and then coat them in the chopped peanuts.
9 Space the balls well apart on the ungreased baking sheet.
10 Flatten the cookies with the prongs of a fork dipped in water.
11 Bake for 10 to 15 minutes.
12 Remove the cookies from the oven and carefully transfer them to a wire cooling rack while still hot.

Get up, brush your teeth and find yourself an elephant

TOP ROW LEFT TO RIGHT: Your muchinda arrives, time to rise and shine; After a successful night of hunting, these lions head for shade; Off we go on a bush walk with Derby, our bushman tracker leading the way. BOTTOM ROW LEFT TO RIGHT: Up close and personal — an elephant bids us good morning; a young bushman devours a wedge of watermelon.

Fresh fruit kebabs

Makes 6

Ingredients
½ Galia, honeydew or watermelon,
 or 1 pineapple, or 2-3 papayas
 plus 2 limes cut into wedges

Special equipment
6 skewers, sticks or twigs

Method
1 Peel the fruit if necessary and cut into large, bite-sized cubes.
2 Thread the fruit onto the skewers, sticks or twigs, placing the lime wedges on last if using.
3 Serve with instructions to squeeze the lime juice over the papaya before eating.

A novel way of presenting fruit kebabs is to cut the fruit into chunks and spike them onto acacia thorns. You can also carve your own kebab sticks from twigs or small branches with a pocketknife. On the early morning safaris we also serve chilled watermelon chopped into wedges with a panga.

Apricot fruit roll

Makes 1 large sheet

Ingredients
Very ripe apricots
White sugar

Special equipment
Food processor
Rolling pin
Wax paper

Method

1 Remove the pits from the apricots and discard.

2 Purée the fruit in the food processor then measure it by volume.

3 To every 1 cup of apricot purée, add the same volume
of sugar and mix well.

4 Spread the purée thinly and evenly onto the wax paper.

5 Carefully place the sheet on a wire rack and leave in the sun for 12 hours
or until dry.

6 Loosen the sheet of fruit from the paper, sprinkle the surface
with a little more sugar and roll up.

Children love these! Any fruit can be used but if you choose peaches, pears
or quinces they will need to be peeled and cooked first. I have also made fruit
roll successfully with dried apricots. Purée about ⅔ cup of ready-to-eat dried
apricots and place the mixture on wax paper lightly sprinkled with sugar. Roll
out thinly and complete as above.

Breakfast in the bush

The lions are still in your thoughts and,

as the Land Rover bounces along, the wonder of the bush unfolds around you. A small herd of zebras gallops off while a few comical wildebeest dash around in circles. Gearing down, your ranger engages a steep, muddy slope and soon you are in a wide riverbed. A herd of buffalo crashes through the reed banks and a crocodile slithers into the water with a furious splash.

Suddenly, you are famished. You had hardly noticed that you have been on the go for almost four hours. Eyes become heavy and heads start to nod as you are rocked into a drowsy slumber by the weaving of the vehicle along the rough, sandy track. Soon after your departure from the lodge the kitchen team and muchindas have been frantic loading the last-minute items onto a vehicle in order to set up a bush breakfast. After a bumpy ride on the back of the kitchen Land Rover, protectively clutching the eggs, they arrive at a site known as "the fig tree." The vehicle is quickly unloaded and the area cleared and checked for any fresh spoor or unwelcome breakfast guests such as lions. First the braais and fires are placed and the logs unloaded. Sticks are gathered to light the fires, the coolers unpacked and the bar set up. A buffet trestle table is laden with muesli, muffins, freshly squeezed juices, jams and a large wooden bowl of fresh fruit. An assortment of carved stools, blankets and large printed cushions are arranged around a central fire.

In the Land Rover, you are wondering about breakfast and how long it will take you to get back to camp. Suddenly, the vehicle stops in the middle of nowhere. The ranger suggests a short walk and heads off along a narrow path into the surrounding bush. You follow, thinking that this had better be good because you are starving. Then, to your utter amazement, there it is: breakfast in the bush! Someone hands you an ice-cold Bloody Mary made from chili vodka and all drowsiness vanishes. On the barrel braais, known as jikkas, there is a cast-iron pot of Amarula maltabella, another pot of simmering water ready to soft-boil the eggs, and some kebabs of bacon-wrapped game sausages threaded with lemon leaves, prunes and bright yellow mealies. You select a delicious homemade muesli with several tasty toppings such as toasted coconut slivers and mixed dried fruits, toasted nuts and yogurt. Thick slices of freshly baked honey bread spread with tropical banana jam are passed around as you happily take a place on one of the ornate African hand-carved stools.

Carrot and pineapple juice

Makes 4½ cups

Ingredients
3lb 5oz carrots
3 pineapples

Special equipment
Juice extractor

Method
1 Peel the carrots and pineapples.
2 Juice them together, transferring the liquid to a large pitcher if necessary.
3 Stir and chill before serving.

Nothing can beat freshly squeezed fruit and vegetable juices.
The combinations are endless — a favorite of mine is carrot and ginger.
Remember, too, that various fruit juices such as melon or pear mixed with
champagne make a wonderful alternative to mimosas.

Chili vodka

Makes 3 cups

Ingredients
1 bottle vodka
3-12 red chilis
Tonic water (optional)

Method
1 Pour yourself a vodka and tonic, creating enough space in the vodka
bottle to add the chilis.
2 Add the chilis according to taste and seal the bottle.
3 Leave for 2 to 3 days before use, but preferably for a week in the freezer.

If taking this out into the bush, place the bottle of chili vodka inside a can or a
narrow plastic container large enough to cover halfway up the bottle. Fill the
container with water and leave it to freeze with the bottle inside. This will
ensure your chili vodka is served ice-cold in the blistering heat.

Chili vodka bloody marys

Serves 8

Ingredients
Cubed or crushed ice
6¼ cups tomato juice
¼ cup Worcestershire sauce
4-8 shots chili vodka
Juice of 3-4 lemons
Celery salt

Method
1 Half fill a pitcher with the ice.
2 Add the tomato juice, Worcestershire sauce, chili vodka and lemon
juice to taste, stirring to combine.
3 Pour the cocktail into tall glasses and sprinkle with celery salt.

We garnish each glass of this rich spicy drink with a porcupine quill that has
a chili spiked on the end. The amount of chili vodka you use depends on the
strength of the vodka and your taste for heat!

Yogurt bowl with fresh berries and lemongrass syrup

Serves 6

Ingredients

6 cups white sugar
12 stalks lemongrass
Plain yogurt
A mixture of fresh seasonal berries, hulled and cleaned

Special equipment
Clean wine bottle with cork

Method

1 To make the syrup, place the sugar and lemongrass in a large saucepan with 5 cups of water and bring to the boil.
2 Simmer for 5 minutes.
3 Allow the syrup to cool, then transfer to a clean wine bottle, cork and chill.
4 To serve, spoon the yogurt into individual serving bowls, top with the fresh berries and drizzle with the lemongrass syrup.

Stored in the refrigerator, the lemongrass syrup will keep for 7 to 10 days.

Dried fruit salad

Serves 6-8

Ingredients
2-3 rooibos or Ceylon teabags
4½ cups boiling water
3 cups mixed dried fruit such as apple, apricots, dates, figs, mango and pears
6 tbsp orange juice
1 vanilla bean, split lengthways
4 star anise
2 sticks cinnamon
Pared zest of 1 lemon
Plain yogurt

Method

1 Make the tea to your preferred strength using the boiling water.
2 Remove the teabags and allow to cool.
3 Place the dried fruit in a bowl and cover with the cold tea.
4 Leave to soak for at least 8 hours.
5 Transfer to a saucepan and add the orange juice, spices and lemon zest.
6 Simmer until the fruits are tender — the length of time will depend on the quality and dryness of the fruit.
7 Serve the fruit salad warm or cold with a little yogurt.

Rooibos tea is harvested from an indigenous red bush that grows in the Western Cape of South Africa. It is also known as "bush tea" and is caffeine free. If you cannot find it, Ceylon tea is a good alternative.

Homemade muesli with various toppings

Makes about 4lb 8oz

Ingredients

For the muesli:
3 cups Shredded Wheat
3 cups rolled oats
1½ cups sunflower seeds
2 cups honey
½ cup sunflower oil
2 tbsp ground cinnamon

For the toppings:
Lightly toasted coconut slivers
Sliced mixed dried fruit, such as
    apples, apricots, dates, figs,
    mangos, peaches, pears and
    raisins
Toasted mixed nuts, such as whole
    almonds, cashews, macadamias
    and pecans
Banana chips
Sliced fresh bananas
Natural yogurt

Special equipment
Large deep roasting pan

Method

1 Preheat the oven 400°F.
2 Crumble the Shredded Wheat into the roasting pan — you want them to fall apart in flakes.
3 Add the rolled oats and sunflower seeds and mix well.
4 In a bowl, combine the honey, sunflower oil and cinnamon.
5 Stir the honey mixture thoroughly into the oat mixture until the cereal and seeds are evenly coated.
6 Bake, stirring occasionally, until the muesli turns golden brown.
7 Allow to cool before storing.
8 Serve with a selection of the toppings offered in separate bowls so that guests can help themselves.

The muesli will keep for a month in an airtight container.

Buttermilk pancakes with cinnamon brown sugar, honey and lemon

Makes 8

Ingredients

¼ cup brown sugar
2 tbsp cinnamon
Honey
1 lemon, cut into wedges

For the pancakes:
2 cups flour
1 tbsp white sugar
1 tsp baking powder
1 tsp baking soda
1 tsp salt
2 eggs
2 cups buttermilk
5 tbsp butter, melted
Oil, for greasing

Method
1 To make the pancakes, sift the dry ingredients together in a large bowl.
2 In a separate bowl, beat together the eggs, buttermilk and melted butter.
3 Make a well in the center of the flour and add the buttermilk mixture.
4 Gradually beat in the flour to give a smooth batter.
5 Heat a small frying pan and brush with a little oil.
6 Ladle a little of the batter into the pan.
7 Cook the pancake until bubbles start to appear on the surface and the underneath is golden brown.
8 Turn the pancake over and cook the other side until golden brown.
9 Set aside in a warm place and repeat with the remaining batter.
10 Divide the pancakes among the serving plates.
11 Combine the brown sugar and cinnamon in a bowl.
12 Sprinkle the cinnamon sugar over the pancakes, drizzle with a spoonful of honey and serve with a lemon wedge.

Whiskied jungle oats with vanilla brown sugar

Serves 2

Ingredients
2¼ -3½ cups milk
1 cup rolled oats
½ tsp salt
4 tbsp whipped cream
4 tbsp vanilla brown sugar
2-4 shots whisky

Method
1 Bring the milk to the boil.
2 Whisk in the rolled oats and cook for 3 to 5 minutes until thick — if you prefer your oatmeal thinner, gradually add more hot milk until the desired consistency is achieved.
3 Spoon into individual serving bowls, place a large dollop of cream in the center of each and sprinkle with the vanilla brown sugar.
4 Drizzle the whisky over the top and serve.

To make vanilla brown sugar, split a vanilla pod in half and place it in a jam jar filled with brown sugar or brown sugar crystals. Leave for several days to allow the flavor to develop. As an alternative to this oatmeal we sometimes serve maltabella, a malted hot cereal made from sorghum, which is one of the staple grains of Africa. Instead of whisky and vanilla brown sugar, we top the maltabella with Amarula, a South African wild fruit cream liqueur made from the fruit of the marula tree, a popular snack with the elephants.

Sweet potato, onion and thyme pancakes

Makes 16

Ingrdients
3 eggs, lightly beaten
½ cup milk
2 tbsp olive oil
1¼ cups flour
12 oz sweet potatoes,
  peeled and coarsely grated
2 onions, thinly sliced
2 tsp dried thyme
Sunflower or peanut oil for frying
Salt and freshly ground pepper

Method

1 Combine the eggs, milk and olive oil in a small bowl.

2 Place the flour in a large bowl and slowly stir in the egg mixture until a smooth batter is formed.

3 Add the sweet potatoes, onions and thyme, season and mix well.

4 Pour a little oil into a frying pan and heat until hot but not smoking.

5 Place a small ladle of the pancake mixture in the frying pan and press into shape, then repeat with more of the mixture until the base of the pan is full.

6 Fry for about 2 minutes on both sides until the pancakes are golden brown.

7 Remove and drain on paper towel before serving.

Beating the heat, time to seek shade

LEFT TO RIGHT: At Makalali, bush breakfasts are served under an enormous wild fig tree; Helen, one of the staff, keeps bugs at bay with a twig; the coffee pot is set to brew over an open fire; grass is harvested by African women during the winter months to make these thatched roofs.

Bacon-wrapped Eland wors with mealies and lemon leaves

Makes 6

Ingredients
3lb 5oz eland wors or
  venison cocktail sausages
24 slices bacon
12 ready-to-eat prunes
3-4 mealies or ears of corn
⅓ cup olive oil
24 lemon or bay leaves
Salt and freshly ground pepper

Special equipment
6 skewers

Method

1 Twist the eland wors or venison sausages into mini-sausages about 2 inches long, and separate — you should have 18 in total.

2 Wrap a slice of bacon around each sausage.

3 Cut the remaining 6 bacon slices in half and wrap them around the prunes.

4 Chop the mealies or corn into 1¼inch pieces.

5 Thread the bacon-wrapped sausages onto the skewers, alternating them with the lemon leaves, bacon-wrapped prunes and mealies or corn — each skewer should end with a sausage.

6 Brush the kebabs with a little olive oil and season with salt and pepper just before cooking.

7 Cook (preferably under a fig tree) on a grate over hot coals, turning occasionally; alternatively, place under a hot broiler and cook for 10 minutes or so, turning occasionally, until the wors is cooked.

We ask the trackers to collect wild raisin bush sticks and carve them into skewers. Alternatively, you can use metal or wooden kebab sticks.

Soft-boiled eggs with harissa

Serves 6

Ingredients
6 eggs
6-12 slices bread
Harissa (see page 19)

Special equipment
6 egg cups

Method

1 To soft-boil the eggs, pierce the rounded end of the shell with a needle and place in a saucepan of water.

2 Bring to the boil and simmer the eggs for 3 to 5 minutes according to your preference.

3 Meanwhile, toast the bread.

4 Drain the eggs and place them in the egg cups.

5 Serve the eggs with the toast, cut into strips, and a little bowl of harissa.

6 To eat, dip the toast strips into the harissa before dipping them in the egg.

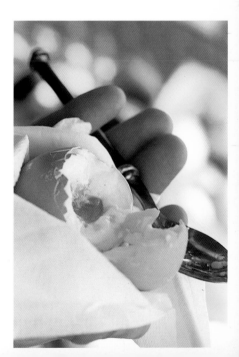

Ethiopian honey bread

Makes 2lb 4oz loaf

Ingredients
1 cup milk
7 tbsp butter, plus extra
   for greasing
½ cup honey
1 egg
1 tbsp ground coriander
1½ tsp salt
½ tsp ground cinnamon
A pinch of ground cloves
5-6 cups bread flour
1 envelope instant dried yeast

Special equipment
Electric mixer with dough hook

2lb 4oz loaf pan, greased

Method

1 In a small saucepan, place the milk with 4 tablespoons of water and heat until lukewarm.

2 Meanwhile, in another small pan, melt the butter.

3 In a small bowl, mix together the honey, egg, ground coriander, salt, cinnamon and cloves.

4 Place 5 cups of the flour and the yeast into the bowl of the mixer.

5 Make a well in the center and pour in the warmed milk, the melted butter and the honey mixture.

6 Use the dough hook to knead the mixture until it forms a ball, adding extra flour if the dough seems too sticky.

7 Continue kneading until smooth and elastic.

8 Remove the dough from the bowl and set aside.

9 Clean the bowl and grease it with butter.

10 Replace the dough and cover with greased plastic wrap or a shower cap.

11 Leave in a warm, draft-free place until the dough has doubled in size, which should take about 60 minutes.

12 Punch the dough down with your fist and knead it again for 1 to 2 minutes.

13 Put the dough into the loaf pan, pressing it down into the corners.

14 Cover the dough as you did before and leave until it has doubled in size and reached the rim of the loaf pan.

15 Meanwhile, preheat the oven to 300°F.

16 Bake the bread in the middle of the oven for 50 to 60 minutes, until the top is crusty and light golden brown and the base sounds hollow when tapped.

17 Remove the bread from the pan and allow to cool on a wire rack.

Traditionally eaten with butter and honey, this makes an excellent breakfast toast and I like to serve it with East African Banana Jam (opposite). Please note that this loaf is cooked at a cooler temperature than other breads.

East African banana jam

Makes 2 cups

Ingredients
1¾ cups sugar
½ cup fresh lemon juice, strained
1 tbsp lemon zest
6 ripe bananas

Special equipment
Preserving pan or large,
  heavy-based saucepan
Sugar thermometer
Canning jar or jam jar
Wide neck metal funnel

Method

1 Put the sugar, lemon juice and zest into a large bowl and stir until the sugar has almost dissolved.

2 Peel and slice the bananas, add them to the lemon mixture and gently stir until they are well coated.

3 Cover the bowl with plastic wrap and leave to marinate for 1 hour.

4 Scrape the banana mixture into the preserving pan and place the sugar thermometer inside.

5 Place the pan over a low heat and bring the mixture to the boil, stirring occasionally to prevent sticking.

6 Boil until the sugar thermometer reaches the jam stage 220°F — it will be a lovely rich amber color.

7 Meanwhile, sterilize the jar by bringing a large saucepan of water to the boil.

8 When the water is boiling, immerse the jar in the water for 1 minute, then remove with tongs and allow it to drain and steam itself dry.

9 Place the funnel in the jar and carefully spoon in the banana jam, filling it right to the top, then cover and store for up to 1 month.

Ranger's breakfast on a shovel

Special equipment
Shovel
Tripod
Wooden prop made from the fork of a branch
Spatula

Method

1 Clean your shovel, making sure it is free from rust, then lightly oil.
2 Gather some wood to make a small fire, placing one end of each piece of wood together to form a pyramid.
3 Place some dry grass or twigs in the center underneath and light.
4 You can start to cook soon after — there is no need to wait for coals, unless you want to toast bread.
5 Place the tripod over the fire.
6 Rest the shovel on the tripod and balance the handle with the wooden prop that has been secured in the ground.
7 Put a little oil on the shovel and proceed to cook your breakfast.

A shovel is an essential tool on any bush vehicle and can be used for anything from digging up burst water pipes to extracting stuck vehicles from the thick Kalahari sand. For Stephan Jooste, one of the Tswalu rangers, it also doubles as a handy frying pan. During the winter months, the Tswalu rangers spend weeks in the bush, herding wild antelope such as oryx, wildebeest and kudu into concealed capture pens with a helicopter before translocating them to other reserves. There are no set eating times for the rangers and any lull in the action is utilized to grab a quick meal and a nap. Stephan is a firm believer in a hearty breakfast and at the first opportunity prepares himself a scrumptious fry-up on a shovel. Although he endured a little envious teasing from the other rangers at first, his ingenious method has become popular and I decided to use it for the guests' breakfasts too.

Traditional fry-up

Serves 2

Ingredients
4 tbsp sunflower oil
2 sausages
1 tomato
2 flat mushrooms
6 bacon slices
2 eggs
Salt and pepper

Method

1 Heat half the oil in a frying pan (or on a spade) over a medium heat.
2 Add the sausages and cook for about 7 minutes, turning regularly until they are evenly browned.
3 While the sausages are cooking, halve and lightly season the tomato and add to the pan with the mushrooms.
4 Cook the tomato and mushrooms for 2 to 3 minutes on both sides.
5 Transfer the cooked sausage, tomato and mushrooms to a warm plate and set aside in a warm place.
6 Add the bacon to the pan and fry it on both sides, then set aside with the other cooked ingredients.
7 Add a little extra oil to the pan if necessary, crack in the eggs and fry them to your liking, then serve with the sausage, tomato, mushrooms and bacon.

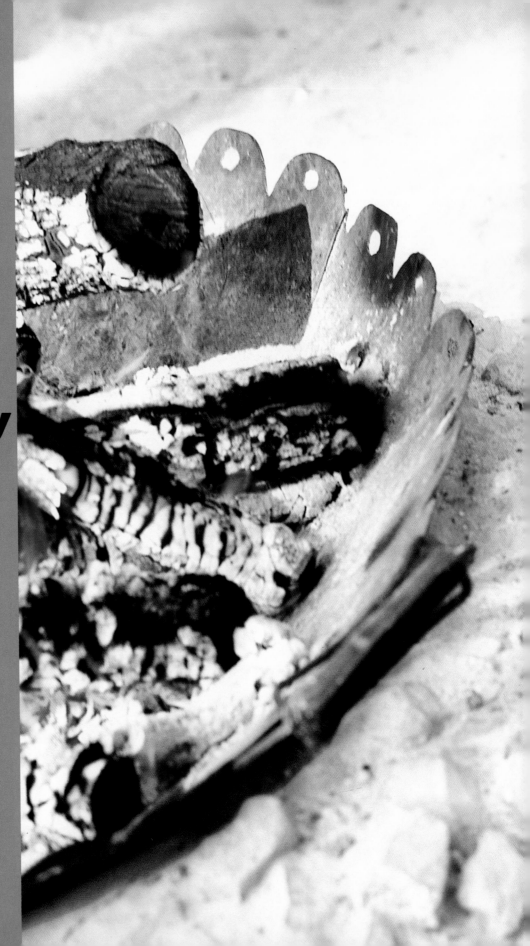

**Lunch
time
everybody**

It is boiling hot and the bush has gone quiet; only the steady buzzing of cicadas breaks the silence. A lonely dust devil dances across the horizon that shimmers in the midday sun. After returning from your game drive, you take the opportunity to cool off with a quick dip in the rock pool, then gracefully accept a large chilled drink from a passing muchinda before reclining in a comfortable hammock in the shade of an acacia tree.

In the kitchen the pace is picking up as the team prepares for lunch. Banana leaves are picked to decorate the big rustic wooden lunch platters. A large bowl of curried apple soup is placed in the fridge to chill and trays of apple slices are gently drying in the oven. One of the chefs is in the shamba, or lodge vegetable garden, choosing the fresh herbs and lettuce for the lunch platters. The clean-up team is hard at it, cleaning the tiles and windows and polishing cutlery and glasses. The weekly deliveries are being checked in and packed away and everyone sighs with relief that the orders are complete so there will not be any frantic last-minute menu changes. Even the eggs survived the rough dirt track. The lunch chef is rehearsing her menu while assembling the platters and some of the team are tasting and commenting on a new salad. The aroma of freshly baked bread permeates the air as, one by one, the loaves are taken out of the oven and placed on cooling racks. There is a small portable radio playing the latest African hits. Some of the chefs are singing along and swaying to the rhythm, their harmonious voices blending in unison with the usual banter and occasional teasing. The assistant chef is teaching the dishwashing staff a new elaborate handshake and they all shriek with laughter.

A singing procession of chefs and muchindas, stylishly adorned in crisp white jackets and African print wrap-arounds, appears near you carrying a board of onion and poppy seed bread, bowls of chilled soup and a carved wooden platter with a riot of colorful salads. The chef introduces herself before describing the lunch menu: "Thinly sliced venison bresaola, grilled sweet potatoes with ginger and lime dressing, a green bean, baby corn, olive and basil salad and roast beet and carrot salad. This is followed by blue cheese, green fig preserve and a thin, crisp bread called shraak." The muchinda offers the wine list.

Warm spicy air, gentle African hospitality and refreshingly crisp food lull you into relaxed contentment. After the meal, you ease back into your hammock under the acacia tree.

Shraak

Makes 16

Ingredients
4¼ cups flour
½ tsp salt

Special equipment
Rolling pin

Method
1 Place the flour and salt in a large bowl and stir in 1 cup plus 2 tbsp of lukewarm water or just enough to form a firm dough.
2 Knead the dough until smooth.
3 Cover and let rest for 30 minutes to make the dough more pliable.
4 Preheat the oven to 400°F.
5 Working on a floured surface, divide the dough into 16 equal pieces and roll them out into thin rounds.
6 Place the rounds on a floured baking sheet and bake for 10 to 12 minutes, or until they puff up and lightly color.

Shraak is a thin, crisp unleavened bread that is great to serve with cheese and pickles, or Ouma Rita's Green Fig Preserve (see page 72).

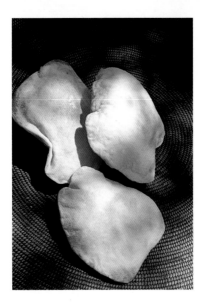

Elephant foot bread

Makes 1 very large loaf

Ingredients
2 cups mashed potato
10½ cups flour, plus extra
for dusting
3 tbsp salt
1 envelope instant dried yeast
5 cups warm water

Special equipment
Electric mixer with large bowl
and dough hook
Large baking tray

Method
1 Place the potato, flour, salt and dried yeast into the mixing bowl and make a well in the center.
2 Pour in the warm water and mix to a dough with the dough hook.
3 Knead the dough until it is smooth and elastic.
4 Shape into a ball and place in a greased bowl.
5 Loosely cover with greased plastic wrap and leave in a warm, draft-free place until the dough has doubled in size.
6 Knock back the dough and knead for 2 to 3 minutes.
7 Shape the dough into a ball, place on a floured baking tray and gently flatten the top a little.
8 With a sharp knife, make two incisions close together on one side of the loaf, then continue cutting along the edge to form the elephant's toenails.
9 Loosely cover the dough with greased plastic wrap and leave to rise in a warm place until the loaf has doubled its size.
10 Meanwhile, preheat the oven to 400°F.
11 Bake for approximately 60 to 75 minutes, or until the loaf sounds hollow when tapped on the bottom.
12 Stand the bread on a wire rack to cool.

This bread, which is made from potato, was one of the first loaves Lori and I taught Julia, who was training to be the baker at Makalali. Julia started working before the camps were open so she would practice making one loaf a day for the staff of about eight. When the lodge opened, I asked Julia to double the recipe. During the morning I happened to be walking by the bread oven and saw an enormous loaf baking. It filled the whole oven! I then realized that I had not explained myself very clearly: I meant for her to double the recipe by making two loaves. Julia was very proud of her huge loaf, went to the camp and introduced it to the guests as elephant foot bread.

Onion and poppy seed bread

Makes 1 large loaf

Ingredients
For the dough:
5¼ cups strong bread flour
1 envelope instant dried yeast
2 tsp salt
1 tsp sugar
1½ cups milk
9 tbsp butter
1 egg, beaten

For the filling:
6 tbsp butter
2 onions, chopped
1 cup feta cheese, crumbled
  (optional)
2-3 sprigs rosemary (optional)
3 tbsp poppy seeds
Salt and freshly ground pepper

For the glaze:
1 egg, lightly beaten
1 tbsp poppy seeds

Special equipment
Electric mixer with dough hook
Rolling pin

Method
1 Place the dry ingredients for the dough into the bowl of the electric mixer and make a well in the center.
2 Put the milk and butter in a saucepan, heat until the butter is melted, then allow to cool until lukewarm.
3 Add the milk mixture and beaten egg to the flour.
4 Using the dough hook, mix together to form a dough.
5 Knead for 6 to 8 minutes until smooth and elastic.
6 Shape the dough into a ball and place in a greased bowl.
7 Lightly cover the dough with greased plastic wrap and place in a warm, draft-free place for about 1 hour or until the dough has doubled in size.
8 To make the filling, melt the butter in a pan and sauté the onions until soft.
9 Remove the onions from the heat and seàson generously.
10 Preheat the oven to 350°F.
11 When the dough has doubled in size, knock it back and knead for 2 or 3 minutes.
12 Place the dough on a floured surface and roll it out into a rectangle about ¼ inch thick.
13 Spread the onion filling over the dough, leaving a border around the edges.
14 Top with the feta cheese and the leaves of the rosemary, if using.
15 Sprinkle the poppy seeds over the other ingredients, then carefully roll up the dough, making sure the filling is enclosed.
16 Place the loaf seam-side down on a floured baking sheet.
17 Lightly cover the loaf with a sheet of greased plastic wrap and leave it to prove for 45 to 60 minutes or until doubled in size.
18 Glaze with the beaten egg and sprinkle with the remaining poppy seeds.
19 Bake for 40 minutes or until the top is golden brown and the base of the loaf sounds hollow when tapped.

Although this rolled loaf is perfectly delicious without cheese and rosemary added to the filling, I suggest you try both versions and see which you prefer. It is excellent with Chilled Curried Apple Soup (see page 58), and makes a good picnic bread when shaped into mini loaves.

Basil and parmesan bread

Makes 2lb 4oz loaf

Ingredients
½ cup milk
2 tbsp butter
2½ cups bread flour
1 envelope instant dried yeast
½ tbsp sugar
A pinch of salt
1 egg, lightly beaten
1 cup parmesan cheese, grated
8 scallions, thinly sliced
1 tsp freshly crushed garlic
12 basil or oregano leaves,
  rolled up tightly and sliced
Salt and freshly ground pepper

Special equipment
Electric mixer with dough hook
  (optional)
2lb 4oz loaf pan

Method
1 Heat the milk in a saucepan with half the butter until it has melted,
then leave to cool until lukewarm.
2 Meanwhile, combine the flour, yeast, sugar and salt in the bowl of the
mixer and make a well in the center.
3 Add the milk mixture, egg and parmesan cheese to the flour.
4 Mix together using the dough hook to form a soft dough.
5 Knead for 6 to 8 minutes with the dough hook until smooth and elastic;
alternatively, place the dough on a well-floured surface and knead by hand
for 8 to 10 minutes.
6 Shape the dough into a ball and place it in a greased bowl.
7 Cover the dough with greased plastic wrap or a shower cap and place in a
warm, draft-free place until it doubles in size, approximately 1 to 1½ hours.
8 Sauté the scallions in a small frying pan with the remaining tbsp of butter
until it is lightly colored.
9 Add the garlic, season with salt and pepper and set aside to cool.
10 Stir the chopped basil or oregano into the scallion mixture.
11 When the dough has doubled in size, knock back the dough and knead
in the cooled onion and herb mixture.
12 Shape the dough into a loaf and place it in the pan.
13 Cover loosely with greased plastic wrap or a shower cap and allow to rise
in a warm place for about 30 minutes or until it has doubled its size again.
14 Meanwhile, preheat the oven to 350°F.
15 Bake for 50 to 60 minutes or until the loaf sounds hollow when tapped.
16 Turn the loaf out onto a wire rack to cool.

Chilled curried apple soup with dried apple rings

Serves 6-8

Ingredients

For the apple rings:
1 Granny Smith apple

For the soup:
1 tbsp butter
1 onion, chopped
1 tbsp mild curry powder
2¼ lbs Granny Smith apples,
    peeled, cored and chopped
4½ cups chicken stock
¾ cup light cream
Juice of 1-2 lemons
Salt and pepper

Special equipment
Food processor
Baking tray with wire rack

Method
1 Preheat the oven to 210°F.
2 Thinly slice the single apple vertically, the thinner the better.
3 Place the apple slices on a wire rack set over a baking tray.
4 Place in the oven to dry for about 30 to 60 minutes, or until the apple slices are completely dry, turning once during cooking.
5 Remove the apple slices from the wire rack and cool on wax paper.
6 To make the soup, in a saucepan, melt the butter and sweat the onion.
7 Add the curry powder and cook for 1 minute.
8 Add the chopped apples, chicken stock and some salt and pepper.
9 Bring the mixture to the boil and simmer covered for about 1 hour.
10 Liquidize the soup, then strain it through a sieve and leave to cool.
11 Add the cream and fresh lemon juice to taste, then adjust the seasoning as necessary.
12 Place the soup in the refrigerator to chill, then serve in chilled bowls with the dried apple slices as a garnish.

Gazpacho with coriander and chili vodka

Serves 6-8

Ingredients
8 tomatoes
1 cucumber
1 red bell pepper
1 yellow bell pepper
2-3 chilis
1 onion
2 garlic cloves, crushed
6¼ cups tomato juice
½ cup olive oil
Juice of 2 lemons
1 tbsp Worcestershire sauce
1 tsp Tabasco sauce
A little tomato paste, to taste
A little sugar, to taste
½ cup plain yogurt (optional)
1 tbsp coriander leaves
¾ cup Chili Vodka (see page 36)
Salt and freshly ground pepper

Special equipment
Food processor
6-8 shot glasses (optional)

Method
1 Use a small sharp knife to score the base of the tomatoes, then cover them with boiling water and leave to stand for 1 minute.
2 Drain the tomatoes, then remove the skins and seeds and chop the flesh.
3 Peel, seed and dice the cucumber.
4 Core and seed the bell peppers and chilis, then finely dice them.
5 Finely chop the onion.
6 In a large bowl, combine the prepared vegetables with the garlic, tomato juice, olive oil, lemon juice, Worcestershire sauce and Tabasco sauce.
7 Purée approximately one-third of the mixture in the food processor and pour it back into the bowl, mixing well.
8 Season the soup to taste — depending on the flavor and sweetness of the tomatoes, you may need to add some tomato paste and a little sugar.
9 Leave to chill for several hours, preferably overnight.
10 Serve in chilled soup bowls with a spoonful of yogurt if desired, some coriander leaves and a shot glass filled with chili vodka.

Serving this gazpacho with chili vodka helps to break the ice at a meal by providing a talking point. You can down the shot in one, or pour it into the soup, adding as little or as much as you like. Gazpacho improves in taste if made the day before and makes a complete meal served with a bread such as Basil and Parmesan Bread (see page 57).

Chilled yellow pepper soup with deep-fried leek

Serves 6-8

Ingredients
6 yellow bell peppers
1 onion, sliced
2 carrots, sliced
2 cloves garlic, crushed
3 tbsp olive oil
5 cups chicken stock
2 cups buttermilk
2-3 leeks
Oil, for deep-frying
Salt and pepper

Special equipment
Food processor
Deep-fryer (optional)

Method

1 Preheat the oven to 400°F.

2 Roast the bell peppers on a baking tray until the skins are charred.

3 Remove the bell peppers from the oven, cover the baking tray with kitchen foil and leave to stand for 15 minutes.

4 Peel off the skins, discard the seeds and ribs and cut the flesh into strips.

5 In a large saucepan or stockpot, sweat the onion, carrots and garlic in the olive oil until soft.

7 Add the strips of bell pepper to the saucepan, cover with the chicken stock, then bring to the boil and simmer for 10 minutes.

8 Liquidize the soup until smooth then leave it to cool.

9 Add 1½ cups of the buttermilk to the cooled soup, season to taste and place in the refrigerator to chill.

10 Meanwhile, julienne the leek by cutting it into fine strips, then thoroughly wash and dry the strips.

11 Heat the oil in the deep-fryer or a large, heavy-based saucepan and fry the leeks until they begin to color.

12 Drain the leek strips on paper towels and season lightly.

13 Serve the cold soup in chilled bowls, drizzle with the remaining buttermilk and top with a little deep-fried leek.

Goreme

Serves 10-12

Ingredients
3 cups feta cheese, crumbled
1½ cups plain yogurt
2 cloves garlic, crushed
1 tsp paprika, plus extra to garnish
½ tsp cayenne
1 tbsp olive oil
Kalamata olives, to garnish
Salt and pepper

Method

1 Place the feta cheese and yogurt in a bowl and, using a fork, mash them together to form a paste.

2 Add the garlic, paprika, cayenne and a little salt and pepper to taste.

3 Spoon the mixture into a serving bowl.

4 Drizzle the goreme with olive oil and garnish with some Kalamata olives and paprika before serving.

This is a spicy cheese purée that can be served as a dip or a spread. Try it with Shraak (see page 55) or raw vegetables such as carrot sticks.

Masai mara

Serves 6-8

Ingredients
8 large red bell peppers
2¼ cups olive oil
12 cloves garlic, sliced
1 cup pecans, toasted
2 cups fresh white
  breadcrumbs
Juice of 4 lemons
4 tsp ground cumin
4 tsp sugar
1-2 tsp finely chopped chili,
  or to taste
Salt and freshly ground pepper

Special equipment
Food processor

Method
1 Preheat the oven to 475°F.
2 Cut the bell peppers in half and remove the seeds and ribs.
3 Using your hands, coat the bell peppers with a little of the olive oil, place them cut-side up on a baking tray and sprinkle with the garlic.
4 Roast until they begin to blacken, then turn over and continue roasting until the other side begins to blacken.
5 When cool enough to handle, remove the skin and cut the flesh into strips.
6 Place the bell peppers, garlic, pecans, breadcrumbs, lemon juice, cumin, sugar, chili and some salt and pepper into the bowl of the food processor and whizz until smooth.
7 Pour in the remaining olive oil and continue processing until the mixture is smooth and glossy.
8 Taste the masai mara and adjust the seasoning, adding plenty of salt to bring out the bold flavors.

Masai mara is delicious spread on freshly baked bread, particularly a loaf made from the buttermilk dough used for Roosterkoek (see page 121).

A busy day out in the bush

TOP ROW LEFT TO RIGHT: A picnic lunch spread under the canopy of a Shepherd's tree — its dried and roasted roots are used as a substitute for coffee; at Jack's Camp, the Lonely Acacia is a typical umbrella thorn found throughout the African savanna; an African decorative motif beneath a thatched roof.
CENTER: A foraging warthog — the female has only one pair of facial warts and smaller tusks than the male.
BOTTOM ROW LEFT TO RIGHT: Salphina carrying her le hudu into the boma to grind peanuts; an elephant in full retreat through the llala palms.

Bresaola-style venison

Serves 6-8

Ingredients

½ tsp coriander seeds
½ tsp cumin seeds
2½ tbsp brown sugar
1 tbsp freshly ground black pepper
½ tsp dried thyme
½ tsp ground ginger
2 juniper berries, crushed
½ tsp freshly grated nutmeg
¼ tsp ground cloves
3 cardamon seeds, finely crushed
2 medium venison fillets, trimmed
4 tsp salt
1 tbsp oil
1 tbsp butter

Method

1 In a dry frying pan, toast the coriander and cumin seeds until fragrant, leave to cool, then grind them to a powder.

2 Mix the coriander and cumin with the brown sugar, black pepper, thyme, ginger, juniper, nutmeg, cloves and cardamon and rub into the venison.

3 Place the fillets in a plastic container, cover and refrigerate for 2 days, turning the meat once each day.

4 On the third day, rub the salt into the fillets.

5 Refrigerate for 8 more days, again turning the meat every day.

6 Heat a large frying pan until it is smoking hot, add the oil and butter and sear the meat on all sides.

7 Allow the venison to cool before slicing it thinly.

Allow 11 days to make this spiced venison fillet — it may seem a long time but it is definitely worth the wait. Remember to turn the meat every day.

Smoked chicken with dried apricots, pistachios and fresh cilantro

Serves 8

Ingredients
1 smoked chicken
¾ cup dried apricots, thinly
sliced
½ cup unsalted pistachios,
coarsely chopped
A small bunch of cilantro,
coarsely chopped
2-3 tbsp olive oil
Salt and freshly ground pepper

Method
1 Remove the chicken flesh from the bone, discarding the skin, and tear the meat into small pieces.
2 In a large bowl, mix together the apricots, pistachios and cilantro, adding just enough olive oil to moisten the salad.
3 Season to taste and serve.

An invention of mine, this recipe was devised because I had a smoked chicken and was not sure what to do with it. The sweetness of the apricots contrasts beautifully with the smokiness of the chicken and the nutty pistachios and the salad is very attractive too. Sometimes I like to use mint instead of cilantro.

Grilled calamari salad with peanuts and chilis

Serves 6-8

Ingredients
¾ cup unsalted peanuts
Juice of 2 lemons
2 tbsp molasses
2 red chilis, finely chopped,
or to taste
2 cloves garlic, crushed
A large bunch of parsley, chopped
A few sprigs of mint, chopped
2¼ lbs calamari tubes
4 tbsp olive oil
Salt and freshly ground pepper

Special equipment
Cast-iron grill pan

Method
1 Mix together the peanuts, lemon juice, molasses, chilis, garlic, parsley and mint, adding the chilis a little at a time until the desired level of heat is obtained, then set aside.
2 Cut open the calamari tubes and scrape clean the insides.
3 Use a sharp knife to score the tubes with a hatch pattern.
4 In a bowl, combine the calamari with the olive oil and some salt and pepper.
5 Heat the grill until very hot.
6 Working in batches, grill the calamari for 2 minutes on each side, pressing the curled edges down with a spatula so they cook evenly.
7 When all the calamari are cooked, toss them with the peanut and chili mixture and season to taste before serving hot or cold.

Cucumber and feta salad
with fennel and mint

Serves 6

Ingredients

2 large cucumbers, quartered and
   sliced ¼-in thick
2 tsp salt
4 tbsp extra virgin olive oil
2 tbsp freshly squeezed lemon juice
9 oz feta cheese, cut into
   large cubes
8 scallions, sliced diagonally
4 tbsp chopped fennel fronds, plus
   a few fronds extra, to garnish
4 tbsp chopped fresh mint, plus a
   few sprigs extra, to garnish
Salt and freshly ground pepper

Method

1 Place the sliced cucumber in a colander, sprinkle it with the salt and leave
for 30 minutes to extract some of the juices.
2 Meanwhile, in a small bowl, make a dressing with the olive oil and lemon
juice, adding salt and pepper to taste.
3 Pat the cucumber dry with paper towels.
4 In a salad bowl, mix together the cucumber, feta cheese, scallions,
chopped fennel and mint.
5 Add the dressing, toss, then taste and adjust the seasoning as necessary.
6 Garnish with the fennel fronds and mint sprigs and serve.

Feta, along with cheddar and gouda, is one of South Africa's most popular
cheeses and easy to find. We pick our fennel and mint from the garden. In
this recipe it is important to salt the cucumber to remove the excess water,
especially if the salad is being made a few hours in advance.

Grilled sweet potato
with ginger and lime dressing

Serves 8

Ingredients

6 small sweet potatoes
1 cup olive oil
⅓ cup fresh lime juice
3 tbsp chopped fresh cilantro
2 tbsp honey
4 tsp grated fresh ginger
1 red chili, seeded and finely
   chopped
2 cloves garlic, crushed
Salt and freshly ground pepper

Special equipment
Cast-iron grill pan

Method

1 Peel the sweet potatoes and thinly slice them horizontally to a thickness
of approximately ⅛ inch.
2 In a large saucepan of boiling water, blanch the sweet potatoes for 1 minute,
then drain and allow the slices to steam dry.
3 Put the sweet potatoes into a bowl, add 4 tablespoons of olive oil and mix
with your hands until the slices are well coated.
4 Heat the grill over a high heat until it begins to smoke.
5 Working in batches, grill the sweet potatoes on both sides until they are well
charred, then place them in a large bowl.
6 To make the dressing, mix all the remaining ingredients together
in a separate bowl and adjust the seasoning to taste.
7 Drizzle the dressing over the grilled sweet potatoes and serve hot or cold.

Roast beet and carrot salad

Serves 6-8

Ingredients
About 3½ lbs beets
4-6 carrots, quartered lengthways
3 tbsp olive oil

For the dressing:
½ cup olive oil
⅓ cup freshly squeezed lemon juice
A bunch of chives, chopped
A small bunch of mint, coarsely
  chopped
1 tbsp ground cumin
1 tbsp paprika
1 clove garlic, crushed
½ tsp honey
Salt and freshly ground pepper

Method
1 Preheat the oven to 350°F.
2 Rub the beets with some of the olive oil and roast until soft — the point of a knife should insert easily when the beets are cooked.
3 Meanwhile, in a separate pan, roast the carrots in the same way.
4 When cool enough to handle, remove the skin from the beets and cut them into bite-sized wedges.
5 Place the beets and carrots together in a bowl.
6 In a small bowl, mix together all the ingredients for the dressing, adding salt and pepper to taste.
7 Pour the dressing over the vegetables, mix well and serve hot or cold.

Beets are a vegetable people often seem to forget about, but there are lots of them in Africa. I prefer to buy them raw, not precooked, then roast them to bring out the naturally sweet flavor.

Green bean salad
with baby corn, basil and black olives

Serves 8

Ingredients
**1lb 5oz green beans,
trimmed**
11½ oz baby corn, trimmed
1 red bell pepper, finely sliced
1 red onion, finely sliced
3 oz Kalamata olives
1 cup extra virgin olive oil
3 tbsp balsamic vinegar
3 tbsp lemon juice
**A small bunch of basil or
marjoram, shredded**
1 tsp crushed garlic
**A little fresh chili, chopped, or
Tabasco or chili sauce, to taste**
Salt and freshly ground pepper

Method
1 Bring a large saucepan of water to boil.
2 Working in batches, blanch the beans for 2 minutes, plunging each batch
into iced water as soon as it is cooked and allowing the cooking water
to return to the boil before continuing.
3 Drain the beans and dry them thoroughly.
4 In a large bowl, combine the beans, baby corn, bell pepper, onion and olives.
5 Add all the remaining ingredients and toss before serving.

One of my favorites, this salad provides a refreshing and crunchy contrast
to the salad of Smoked Chicken with Dried Apricots, Pistachios and Fresh
Coriander (see page 65). Whether or not I use basil or marjoram depends
on how much we have in the garden — the dish would work just as well with
oregano or flat-leaf parsley. Purple basil would be pretty too. In the Kalahari
purple basil and purple sage tend to turn green in summer because the climate
is so hot, but they turn purple again in winter.

Jeanette's charkalaka

Serves 6-8

Ingredients
1 onion, sliced
2 cloves garlic, crushed
1-2 chilis
½ cup olive oil
1 green bell pepper, sliced
1 red bell pepper, sliced
1 yellow bell pepper, sliced
1⅛ lb white cabbage, sliced
1⅛ lb carrots, grated
1 tbsp cayenne pepper
1 tbsp paprika
14½ oz canned peas
Salt and freshly ground pepper

Method
1 Sauté the onion, garlic and chili together until the onion starts to color.
2 Add the bell peppers and cook for 2 to 3 minutes.
3 Add the cabbage, carrots, cayenne and paprika, plus some salt and pepper, and continue cooking until the vegetables are tender.
4 Add the drained peas, remove from the heat and leave to stand before serving either warm or cold.

Charkalaka is reminiscent of a spicy coleslaw. The ingredients are all readily available and inexpensive. A good accompaniment to braaied or cold roast meats, charkalaka is very popular in Africa, where it is served at weddings and parties and even sold canned in the supermarkets. This is a Tswana recipe given to me by Jeanette Pulane Tanke, a chef at Tswalu.

MaJos Jos's charkalaka

Serves 6

Ingredients
1⅔ lbs carrots, grated
½ - 1 chili, or to taste
2 tbsp olive oil
14½ oz canned baked beans
½ cup mayonnaise
Salt and freshly ground pepper

Method
1 Sauté the carrots and chili in the oil until soft.
2 Allow to cool slightly before adding the baked beans and mayonnaise.
3 Season to taste and serve.

A creamier version of charkalaka, this easy recipe came from Josephine Onewang, who was a chef at Tswalu Desert Reserve.

Mango, cucumber and melon salad with toasted sesame seeds

Serves 6

Ingredients
3 tbsp sesame seeds
2 ripe mangoes, peeled and cut into chunks
1 large cucumber, halved, seeded and sliced ⅛ in thick
¼ canteloupe or rockmelon, peeled and cut into chunks
2¼ cups plain yogurt
1 tsp cider vinegar
Salt and freshly ground pepper

Method
1 In a dry frying pan, toast the sesame seeds over a medium heat, stirring constantly, until lightly browned, then set aside to cool.
2 Combine the mangoes, cucumber and melon in a bowl.
3 Stir in the yogurt, vinegar and sesame seeds.
4 Season to taste with salt and pepper and serve.

Easy combinations go down well in the heat and this is a particularly light and refreshing summertime dish. Fruit is frequently used in salads in Africa.

Green lentil and banana salad

Serves 8

Ingredients
2 cups green lentils
3 tbsp olive oil
1 onion, chopped
1 red bell pepper, diced
1 tbsp crushed garlic
3-4 semi-ripe bananas, peeled
  and sliced
4 tbsp balsamic vinegar
3 tbsp coarsely chopped cilantro
2 tbsp chopped parsley leaves
Salt and freshly ground pepper

Method
1 Place the lentils in a saucepan, cover generously with water, bring to a boil and simmer until just tender.
2 Drain the lentils and transfer them to a mixing bowl to cool.
3 In a frying pan, heat the olive oil and sauté the onion, bell pepper and garlic for about 2 minutes or until soft.
4 Add the onion mixture to the cooled lentils.
5 Carefully stir the bananas, vinegar and herbs into the lentils.
6 Adjust the seasoning to taste and chill before serving.

Lentils are widely available, inexpensive and easy to store so they are a good ingredient to have delicious recipes for. Here their nutty flavor contrasts well with the sweetness of the soft banana and piquant balsamic vinegar. Serve this salad with a smoked fish such as tuna or butterfish.

Watermelon and pineapple salad

Serves 6

Ingredients
1lb 2oz watermelon, cut into
  bite-sized chunks
1lb 2oz pineapple, cut into
  bite-sized chunks
1 onion, thinly sliced
1-2 tbsp cilantro
6 tbsp lime juice
2 tbsp red wine vinegar
Freshly ground pepper

Method
1 Place the fruit, onion, cilantro, lime juice and red wine vinegar in a bowl.
2 Toss, add pepper to taste, then chill before serving.

Usually people serve watermelon simply as a fruit, but they are so big and we have so many of them in Africa that I wanted to develop more ways of serving them. This type of savory fruit salad suits the African climate. It is delicious served with the Green Bean Salad with Baby Corn, Basil and Black Olives (see page 69), or with Grilled Calamari Salad with Peanuts and Chilis (see page 65). I also suggest you try it with ham or braised pork.

Ouma Rita's green fig preserve

Makes four 18floz jars

Ingredients
2lb 4oz green figs
7¼ cups sugar
1 small ginger root, bruised
4 tsp fresh lemon juice

Special equipment
4 x 18floz canning jars

Method
1 Scrape the figs lightly with a knife to remove the fluff on the skin, then make a small cross on the rounded bottom of each fig.
2 Place figs in 2¼ quarts of water and leave to soak overnight.
3 Drain and rinse the figs thoroughly in fresh water.
4 Place the figs in a bowl, cover with fresh water and leave them to soak for another 15 minutes.
5 Drain the figs, place in a saucepan and cover completely with fresh water.
6 Bring to the boil and cook for about 15 minutes or until tender.
7 Drain the figs, reserving the cooking liquid, and set aside to cool.
8 Put the sugar, ginger root, lemon juice and 2 quarts of the cooking liquid into a large saucepan.
9 Stir the mixture until the sugar dissolves and then bring to the boil.
10 Squeeze the excess water from the figs and place them one at a time in the boiling syrup, ensuring that the syrup does not stop boiling.
11 Boil the figs, uncovered, until they are tender and translucent and the syrup has thickened to a syrup.
12 Meanwhile, sterilize the canning jars.
13 Remove the ginger root from the saucepan, then spoon the hot figs and syrup into the jars, filling to the brim and sealing immediately.

My late grandmother-in-law, who was Afrikaans, used to serve this with cheese, bread, preserved watermelon and preserved ginger.

Afternoon refreshments

You wake from a siesta feeling drowsy and contented.

The intense heat of the day is over and, as the shadows get longer, the bush starts to stir again. Down at the waterhole a family of warthogs is rolling in the sticky black mud and doves are cooing soothingly in the trees behind your tent. A quick shower leaves you feeling wonderfully refreshed and relaxed. Everyone has been asked to meet the ranger on the lodge deck for afternoon tea before the evening game drive.

In the kitchen the pace has slowed down slightly; it is a restful time in the lodge. The evening chefs take this opportunity for a well-deserved break, while the pastry chef meticulously cuts out the scones, places them on a baking tray and slides them into the oven. The muchindas are out on the deck setting up the afternoon tea station with coffee, iced rooibos and mango tea and pitchers of homemade lemonade. The urns in the kitchen are filled and set to boil.

The rangers and trackers are busy refuelling and preparing their vehicles. Spare tires, hi-lift jacks, first aid kits, rifles, spotlights, binoculars and reference books are all stowed and secured with the ease of practiced familiarity. Coolers and green canvas hot boxes are dragged into the kitchen to be refilled with spicy snacks and refreshing drinks for the afternoon's journey through the veld. Routes for the evening game drive are discussed and the trackers are given final instructions on departure times.

Meanwhile, the kitchen staff are all crowding around the baking section to learn how to make a piping bag. These will be used to draw lion paw prints onto a tray of rich chocolate brownies. The first hesitant attempts are accompanied by shrieks of laughter and teasing, but as the chefs become more confident, it becomes a competition to see who can pipe the best paw print. As teatime draws near, orange and lemon zests are caramelized to decorate the poppy seed cake and the pastry chef proudly removes a steaming tray of light scones from the oven. She then slices some biltong and sprinkles it over the roast vegetable pizzas before drizzling them liberally with spicy Moroccan harissa paste.

Out on the deck, the rangers greet their guests and introduce the new arrivals. The ranger gives a brief description of the afternoon drive and what to expect as a muchinda offers you yet another delicious scone dripping with melted butter and banana jam. After a cup of steaming tea, or perhaps another cooling lemonade, you are raring to go again.

How to build a pizza oven out of a termite mound in under 2 hours

Special equipment
Vacated termite mound
Brandy and Coke
Panga or large and threatening saw/hoe-type thing
Shovel
Two hands
Water
Wood
Matches
Appetite
Edouardo Jalapeño

Time plan
½ hour to build oven
1 hour to get fire started and to the correct temperature
2 minutes to cook pizza
3 seconds to eat it

1 Locate in your neighborhood a vacated (very important) termite mound of the correct size and shape, ensuring it has not been blemished in any way by an aardvark.

2 Check the surrounding area for any dangerous animals — specifically predators, but also anything with a trunk and tusks.

3 Hand the brandy and Coke, panga and shovel to Edouardo Jalapeño and take a seat while he proceeds to knock a hole in exactly the right spot on the termite mound, as if he and his ancestors had been doing it for centuries.

4 Use the water to turn the soil from the mound into mud, then use this mixture to level out and seal the base of the oven.

5 Leave to dry — at midday in Botswana, this takes seconds.

6 Find the firewood and build the fire in the now-dry oven.

7 Light it, then step back to admire — the fire is ready when the coals are white and make your hand burn in under 10 seconds.

8 Remove the brandy and Coke from Edouardo and get him to push the coals to the side of the oven: you are now ready to begin cooking.

Roast vegetable pizzas with biltong and harissa

Makes 6

Ingredients

For the pizza base:
5 cups flour, plus extra for dusting
1 envelope instant dried yeast
1½ tsp salt
1⅓ cups lukewarm water
2 tbsp Berbere (see page 18)

For the topping:
1 butternut squash, peeled
  and cubed
1 eggplant, cubed
½ head garlic, cloves separated
1 onion, cut into wedges
1 red bell pepper, seeded and cut
  into large pieces
3 zucchinis, thickly sliced
  horizontally
3 tbsp olive oil
7 oz Biltong (see page 19)
6 tbsp Harissa (see page 18)
Salt and freshly ground pepper

Method

1 To make the pizza bases, place the flour, dried yeast and salt in a large mixing bowl and make a well in the center.
2 In another bowl, combine the water, oil and berbere and stir into the flour.
3 Knead to form a dough and continue kneading until smooth and elastic.
4 Place the dough into a greased bowl and lightly cover with a piece of greased plastic wrap or a shower cap.
5 Leave the dough in a warm, draft-free place until it has doubled in size.
6 Preheat the oven to 350°F.
7 To prepare the topping, place the vegetables in a roasting pan, lightly coat with a little olive oil and season.
8 Roast the vegetables for about 30 minutes or until they begin to color.
9 Remove from the oven and allow to cool.
10 To make the pizzas, heat the oven to 400°F and place a heavy baking sheet inside to heat up.
11 When the dough has doubled in volume, knock it back, then divide it into 6 pieces, keeping them covered.
12 On a floured surface, roll the dough out thinly into discs, keeping the unrolled dough covered.
13 Brush each pizza base with a little olive oil and arrange some of the roasted vegetables on top.
14 Lightly flour the preheated tray. Then, working in batches if necessary, carefully place the pizzas on the tray and cook until the bases are crisp.
15 When nearly cooked, sprinkle a few pieces of biltong on top of the pizzas and continue baking for 1 to 2 minutes.
16 Remove the pizzas from the oven and drizzle with harissa.
17 Repeat with the remaining ingredients and serve hot or cold.

Not a run-of-the-mill pizza, this recipe is good for afternoon tea as well as packed lunches or as a snack with evening cocktails. The crispy base is spiced with berbere, which gives a fantastic flavor and eliminates the need for cheese. Any vegetables suitable for roasting can be included, so use whatever you have available. The pizza also works fine without the chewy biltong, but I like to use it because Afrikaans love their meat.

Orange and lemon poppy seed cake

Serves 12

Ingredients

For the cake:
9 tbsp butter, plus extra for
   greasing
1 cup superfine sugar
4 eggs, beaten
2⅔ cups flour
2½ tsp baking powder
¾ cup milk
2 oz poppy seeds
Finely grated zest of 1 orange
Finely grated zest of 1 lemon
2 tsp vanilla extract

For the decoration:
Pared zest of 1 orange, cut into
   thin strips
Pared zest of 1 lemon, cut into
   thin strips
½ cup orange juice
4 tbsp lemon juice
½ cup sugar

Special equipment
8in spring-form cake pan

Method
1 Preheat the oven 300°F.
2 Grease the cake pan and line it with wax paper.
3 Cream the butter and sugar together until light and fluffy.
4 Gradually add the beaten eggs.
5 Sift together the flour and baking powder.
6 Fold the flour into the butter mixture, alternating with the milk.
7 Fold in the poppy seeds, orange and lemon zests and the vanilla.
8 Spoon the cake mixture into the prepared cake pan and bake for
one hour or until a skewer inserted in the center comes out clean.
9 Meanwhile, to make the decoration, blanch the orange and lemon
strips in a small pan of boiling water for 1 minute, then drain.
10 Place the juices and sugar together in a saucepan and stir over
a low heat until the sugar has dissolved.
11 Bring the syrup to the boil and simmer for 5 minutes.
12 When the cake is cooked, remove it from the oven and prick several
holes in the top using a skewer.
13 Pour the hot syrup over the hot cake and neatly arrange the strips
of orange and lemon zest on top.
14 Leave the cake to cool completely before removing it from the pan.

Josie's scones

Makes 8

Ingredients
⅓ cup golden raisins (optional)
½ cup muscadel wine (optional)
4½ cups self-rising flour,
   plus extra for dusting
9 tbsp butter, cubed
1 tbsp sugar
1 tsp salt
2 eggs
1 cup plain yogurt

Special equipment
Food processor
Cookie cutter

Method
1 If using the golden raisins and muscadel, soak them together for 2 hours.
2 Preheat the oven to 400°F.
3 Place the flour, cubed butter, sugar and salt in a food processor
and process until the mixture resembles fine breadcrumbs.
4 In a bowl, beat the eggs and mix in the yogurt.
5 Add the yogurt mixture to the food processor, along with the soaked golden
raisins if using, and pulse until just combined.
6 Place the mixture on a floured surface and knead lightly.
7 Gently flatten out the mixture until it is about 1-inch thick.
8 Dip the cutter into a little flour then cut the dough into scones.
9 Arrange the scones side by side on a floured baking tray, place them
in the oven and bake for 20 minutes until risen and lightly browned.
10 Remove from the oven and allow the scones to cool before cutting
them in half and serving with butter and jam.

Chocolate brownies with lion paw print

Makes 12

Ingredients

For the brownies:
12 eggs
3½ cups brown sugar
4 tsp vanilla extract
1lb 5oz plain chocolate
1¾ sticks butter
¾ cup pecan nuts, coarsely
   chopped
3½ cups self-rising flour, sifted

For the topping:
12oz dark chocolate
1½ cups heavy cream

For the lion paw prints:
3oz dark chocolate
3oz white chocolate

Special equipment
16x12in baking pan,
   greased and lined with wax paper
A drawing or picture of a lion paw
   print, about 1½in
2 paper piping bags

Method
1 Preheat the oven to 350°F.
2 Whisk together the eggs, sugar and vanilla until thick and creamy.
3 Melt the chocolate and butter together, then fold into the egg mixture.
4 Fold in the pecan nuts, then the sifted flour.
5 Pour the mixture into the baking pan and bake for about 45 minutes
or until a crust forms on top and the brownies are slightly soft in the middle.
6 Set the pan on a wire rack and leave the brownies to cool completely.
7 To make the topping, melt the dark chocolate and cream together.
8 Whisk the mixture until it just begins to thicken, then immediately pour
over the chocolate brownies, tilting the pan so that they are evenly covered.
9 Leave the brownies to set in the refrigerator.
10 To make the chocolate lion paw prints, melt the chocolates separately
and pour each one into a piping bag.
11 Place a sheet of wax paper over the drawing of the lion paw.
12 Using the white chocolate, carefully pipe around the outline of the lion
paw and then fill in the paw pads.
13 Use the dark chocolate to pipe a border around the white paw print
and carefully fill in the gaps between the pads.
14 Repeat until you have 12 paw prints, then transfer the whole sheet
of paper to a tray and place in the refrigerator to set.
15 When ready to serve, cut the brownies into portions, peeling the wax
paper away from the bottom, and place on a serving plate.
16 Carefully peel the wax paper away from the chocolate paw
prints and place one on top of each brownie.

Take a walk on the wild side

TOP ROW LEFT TO RIGHT: A guinea fowl feather, and porcupine quills collected on a bush walk; the well utilized llala palm — its hard nuts are carved into vegetable ivory, the leaves are harvested for weaving and the sap is tapped for brewing into llala palm wine; a desert sentinel, the quiver tree has adapted to its harsh desert environment. BOTTOM LEFT: Feeling the heat, even elephants take an afternoon dip.

Lemon and cumin cookies

Makes 30

Ingredients
1¼ cups superfine sugar
9 tbsp butter
2 egg yolks
Finely grated zest of 2 lemons
4 tbsp freshly squeezed lemon juice
2 tsp ground cumin
2½ cups flour
1 tsp baking soda

Method
1 Cream the sugar and butter together until light and fluffy.
2 Gradually beat in the egg yolks, lemon zest, juice and cumin.
3 Sift together the flour and baking soda, then fold into the butter mixture to form a soft dough.
4 Place the dough on a sheet of wax paper and roll into a cylinder about 2 inches in diameter, twisting the ends of the paper together and being careful not to wrap any of the wax paper into the dough.
5 Place in the freezer until the dough is hard.
6 Preheat the oven to 325°F and line a baking sheet with a piece of wax or parchment paper.
7 Unwrap the dough and cut it into ¼-inch thick slices.
8 Place the slices on the baking sheet, leaving a generous space between them to allow for spreading.
9 Bake the cookies for 10 minutes or until firm to touch.
10 Slide the cookies onto a wire rack and leave to cool before serving.

Homemade lemonade

Makes 6¼ cups

Ingredients
4 cups freshly squeezed
  lemon juice
3-3½ cups sugar
Chilled soda water or mineral water,
  to serve
1 lemongrass stalk
1 sprig mint

Special equipment
2 x 1¾ pint bottles with screwcaps
  or corks, sterilized

Method
1 Place the lemon juice and sugar in a saucepan and set over a low heat, stirring constantly until the sugar has dissolved but do not allow it to boil.
2 Strain the mixture, pour it into the bottles and chill until ready to serve.
3 In a serving pitcher, dilute the syrup to taste with soda water, or sparkling or still mineral water.
4 Garnish with the lemongrass and mint and serve.

Homemade lemonade goes down very well with guests because it is highly refreshing and not too sweet. The syrup is good to make when you have a glut of lemons and can be conveniently stored in the fridge for over a month, provided the bottle is sterilized. Try this recipe with clementines, grapefruit, limes or oranges if you prefer, adding less sugar if the fruit is sweet. The syrup can also be used in cocktails, perhaps as a mixer with gin.

Iced rooibos and forest fruit tea

Makes about 17 cups

Ingredients
2 rooibos teabags
1 Ceylon teabag
1 forest fruit teabag
4 cups boiling water
1 cup sugar
4 tsp honey
8 cups cold water
8 cups ice cubes
3 tbsp freshly squeezed lemon juice
1 lemon, sliced
1 orange, sliced

Method
1 Place the teabags in a teapot or pitcher and cover with the boiling water.
2 Brew the tea for 2 minutes then remove the teabags.
3 Dissolve the sugar and honey in the hot tea.
4 Add the cold water, ice and lemon juice to taste.
5 Serve in a pitcher with the lemon and orange slices.

Rooibos tea is available at most health food stores. This drink and the one below will keep for several days in the refrigerator.

Iced rooibos and mango tea

Makes 3¼ cups

Ingredients
2 rooibos teabags
2¼ cups boiling water
1 cup mango juice
2 tsp honey
Ice cubes

Method
1 Place the rooibos teabags in a pitcher and pour in the boiling water.
2 Allow to infuse for 2 to 3 minutes.
3 Remove the teabags, stir in the honey and leave to cool.
4 Add the mango juice and sweeten the mixture further if necessary.
5 Pour the cool tea over ice and serve.

Game drive
and
sundowners

You have an excellent view of the surrounding bush from your vantage point on the open Land Rover as it bumbles down the sandy track. After the heat of the day it is nice to feel the cooler evening air. You pass some elephants browsing under the llala palms, totally oblivious to your presence. A few minutes later the tracker points out some rare white rhino tracks and shows how to identify and age them. He digs up an interesting root and explains its medicinal uses, then picks a wild aromatic herb that he claims can cure anything from malaria to a bad hangover. There are giraffe, stately and elegant, on the horizon as daylight turns to dusk when the smoldering sun touches the earth. The sky, a riot of vivid oranges, mauves and pinks, is unlike anything you have ever witnessed.

The ranger stops the vehicle again and offers a cocktail. You are looking forward to a refreshing drink and opt for a traditional dawa as you gradually stretch your legs. Skillfully the ranger crushes the ice taken from the cooler into a tumbler. He cuts a wedge of lime on a small wooden board on the hood of the Land Rover before adding it to the ice. Vodka is splashed in, then with a wooden stick he twirls in some honey and crushes the lime to release its flavor. The result is a wonderfully refreshing East African cocktail. A can of beet crisps with dukkah is offered around, as well as some droewors and biltong. These air-dried meats were traditionally eaten by early pioneers to supplement fresh rations—today they are considered delicacies.

Meanwhile, back at the camp, the rooms are being cleaned for your return and the kitchen staff are preparing for the evening meal. The wooden boma enclosure is neatly raked and paraffin lanterns are filled and strategically placed. The braai fires are lit well ahead of dinner so that there are plenty of coals ready for cooking the meal. The bar is set up and waiters lay the table settings before the afternoon shift hands over to the evening chefs. Marinated meat is taken out of the fridge and turned for the last time, vegetables are placed in wooden bowls, ready to be taken into the boma, and peri-peri butter is melted for the shrimp kebabs.

Dusk is sudden. Packing up the drinks, the tracker connects a spotlight to the battery and as you head back for camp, eyes glow in the lamplight. Jackals yelp in the distance, crickets come alive and a nightjar flies up from the sandy track. On the western horizon, the evening star shines brightly. The air turns chilly, so you snuggle into the blanket as your eyes search for nocturnal animals such as aardvark, porcupines or possibly even a leopard.

Do-it-yourself popcorn with chili oil

Serves 4

Ingredients
2 oz popping corn
Salt

For the chili oil:
½ cup sunflower oil
3-5 fresh chilis, or to taste

Special equipment
Large lidded pot

Method
1 To make the chili oil, warm the oil in a saucepan and add the chilis.
2 Leave to cool; then pour into a bottle and leave for 2 to 3 days before use.
3 To cook the popcorn, cover the bottom of a large pot with a few tablespoons of the chili oil.
4 Add enough popcorn to cover the bottom of the pot in a single layer.
5 Cover with a lid and place the pot over a medium heat.
6 Allow the corn to pop, shaking the pot from time to time.
7 As soon as the popping has come to a halt, remove the pot from the heat.
8 Carefully remove the lid and season to taste with salt before passing around.

This is called do-it-youself popcorn because the kitchen packs all the ingredients plus the equipment into a hot box for the ranger to cook on the drinks stop.

Spicy fruit and nuts

Serves 6-8

Ingredients
4 tbsp olive oil
½ cup dried dates, pitted
⅓ cup dried apricots
½ cup almonds, whole, unblanched
½ cup cashew nuts
½ cup macadamia nuts, halved
½ cup pecans, halved
Finely grated zest of 1 lemon or lime
2-3 tablespoons coriander leaves
1 red chili, deseeded and finely chopped
Salt and pepper

Special equipment
Large frying pan

Method
1 Warm the oil in the frying pan over a medium heat.
2 Add all the dried fruit and nuts and toss until the apricots and nuts begin to color.
3 Remove from the heat and add the lemon or lime zest, coriander leaves and chili.
4 Mix thoroughly, season to taste and serve straight from the pan.

Here is another dish that can easily be cooked outdoors over a fire. Alternatively, we prepare it in advance and take it on the game drive to enjoy with evening drinks.

Salted almonds and dried mango

Serves 6-8

Ingredients
1½ cups whole almonds
2 tsp salt
5 oz dried mango

Method
1 Preheat the oven to 350°F.
2 Roast the almonds until they are light golden brown.
3 Dissolve the salt in ¼ cup of water and sprinkle the solution over the hot almonds.
4 Stir the almonds to ensure they are evenly coated.
5 Return the nuts to the oven for 2 to 3 minutes to dry them out.
6 Serve the salted almonds and dried mango in separate containers.

A wonderful combination, this recipe contrasts the saltiness of the roast almonds with sweet and chewy dried mango, which is now available at most supermarkets and health food stores.

Roast peanuts in river sand

Serves 6-8

Ingredients
6-8 handfuls unshelled peanuts

Special equipment
Open fire or barbecue
About 12 handfuls clean river sand
Large frying pan (not non-stick)

Method
1 Light the fire or barbecue.
2 Put the clean river sand in the frying pan with the peanuts and place over the fire, allowing the sand to heat up.
3 Frequently toss the nuts in the sand while roasting, cracking open a peanut from time to time to taste if they are roasted sufficiently — be careful as they will soon over-cook and taste bitter.
4 Carefully transfer the peanuts to a bowl or basket and serve hot.

Parsnip and beet crisps with dukkah

Serves 6-8

Ingredients

For the dukkah:
3 cups sesame seeds
2 cups coriander seeds
¾ cup whole hazelnuts
1 cup cumin seeds
1 tsp salt
Dried mint, to taste
Freshly ground black pepper

For the crisps:
4 medium parsnips
6 beets
Vegetable oil, for deep-frying

Special equipment
Mortar and pestle or spice grinder
Mandolin
**Deep-fryer or large, heavy-based
  saucepan**

Method
1 Preheat the oven to 350°F.
2 To make the dukkah, in separate baking pans, roast all the seeds
and nuts until light golden brown, then allow them to cool.
3 Crush them together finely — if using a spice grinder, be careful
not to over-grind; otherwise the nuts will go oily.
4 Add the salt, mint and pepper to taste and store in an airtight container.
5 To make the crisps, peel the vegetables, keeping them separate.
6 Very thinly slice the parsnips horizontally along the length of the vegetable,
preferably using a mandolin, and thinly slice the beets.
7 Heat the oil and deep-fry the parsnip slices in batches until light golden,
placing each batch to drain on paper towels.
8 Sprinkle the parsnips with dukkah while hot.
9 Fry the beet slices in the same way — they tend to burn easily so you may
have to lower the heat a little.
10 Drain the beet slices, sprinkle with dukkah and serve immediately,
or store in an airtight container for 1 to 2 days.

Dukkah is pronounced "dookah." It is a dry mixture of nuts and spices,
traditionally eaten on bread that has first been dipped in olive oil. I like
to serve it as a seasoning on deep-fried vegetable crisps. Stored in an
airtight container, the dukkah will keep for a couple of weeks.

Mantecaos

Makes 30

Ingredients
**1¼ sticks butter
2 cups cheddar cheese,
  coarsely grated
2 cups flour
1 egg yolk
½ tsp salt
2 tsp cumin seeds
A pinch of cayenne pepper
A few pinches of paprika**

Special equipment
Food processor

Method

1 Preheat the oven to 350°F and line a baking sheet with wax or parchment paper.

2 Place all the ingredients except the paprika in a food processor.

3 Pulse the mixture in quick, short spurts until it resembles coarse breadcrumbs, being careful not to over-work the mixture.

4 Roll a little of the mixture into a ball, place it on the baking sheet and flatten slightly with your fingers.

5 Repeat with the remaining mixture.

6 Bake for 10 to 12 minutes or until light golden and slightly puffed.

7 Sprinkle the crackers with paprika and allow them to cool completely on the baking sheet before serving.

These spicy cheese crackers are from North Africa and can be eaten on their own or served with a dip such as Masi Mara (see page 61).

Return to base camp as the sun slowly sets

TOP ROW LEFT TO RIGHT: An elephant foraging beneath the llala palms; Josie and Madida, her Jack Russell, heading home from work; a solitary bull giraffe looks out over a Kalahari sand dune. CENTER: A thunderstorm brewing in the Kalahari, where the storms are short and dramatic. BOTTOM ROW LEFT TO RIGHT: llala palms in Botswana silhouetted against the setting sun; Jaco looks for tracks in a sea of bushman grass.

Mud in your eye (or sand in Jan's eye)

Serves 6-8

Ingredients
Freshly squeezed juice of 2 melons
1 bottle champagne or dry
  sparkling wine, chilled
Ice cubes (optional)

Method
1 Half-fill the glasses with melon juice.
2 Top up with the champagne or sparkling wine, adding ice if desired, and serve the drinks immediately.

This recipe was one of the last ones to be photographed at Jack's Camp in Botswana. It was the beginning of a rainstorm and the migration of zebra and wildebeest to the Makgadikgadi Salt Pan had just begun. During the shoot the wind picked up and Jan got sand in her eye, hence the alternative name.

Imfulafula

Makes 12 pints

Ingredients
1 large pineapple
8 quarts lukewarm water
2¼ cups white sugar
A handful of black or golden raisins
1 envelope instant dried yeast

Special equipment
Large bowl or bucket
Plastic container with a screw cap

Method
1 Peel the pineapple; then wash the skin well and roughly chop it.
2 In the large bowl or bucket, mix together the pineapple skin, lukewarm water, sugar and raisins.
3 Sprinkle in the yeast, without stirring, and let stand for 30 minutes.
4 Stir well, then cover with a clean cloth and leave in a cool place for 1 day.
5 Strain the mixture through cheesecloth and pour into the clean plastic container.
6 Let stand uncovered for another 12 hours.
7 Cap the beer and use within 2 days.

Sipho, a Zulu chef at Phinda Forest Lodge, told me that this pineapple beer is known to his people as Imfulafula, which when translated means River River. It has been given this name because apparently after drinking a couple of glasses you have the courage to cross any flowing river. Hluhluwe is one of the main pineapple producing areas in South Africa and some of the farms border the Phinda lodge. Be careful that the imfulafula doesn't explode on you: it did on me the first time I made it!

Dawa

Serves 4

Ingredients
1 lime, cut into wedges
Crushed ice
8 shots vodka
1 jar clear honey

Special equipment
4 sticks or pieces of dowel

Method
1 Place a lime wedge in each glass and fill three-quarters full with crushed ice.
2 Pour a double shot of vodka into each glass.
3 Dip the sticks into the honey jar and twirl some honey around each stick.
4 Place the sticks in the glasses and serve immediately.

Dawa is a wonderful Kenyan drink, named after the Swahili word for medicine. The idea is to mix your own, by adding the honey and extracting the lime juice with a stick. Be warned: it soon catches up on you.

Ginger beer

Makes 10 pints

Ingredients
9 oz fresh ginger, sliced and
   bruised
2¼ cups sugar
A handful of raisins
1 envelope instant dried yeast

Special equipment
Bottles with screw-top lids,
   sterilized

Method
1 In a large pot, bring 10 pints of water to the boil.
2 Add the ginger and sugar then let cool until lukewarm.
3 Add the raisins and sprinkle in the yeast.
4 Cover and leave in the refrigerator for 2 days.
5 Strain the liquid and pour into the sterilized bottles.
6 Screw on the bottle tops and refrigerate for another 2 days before drinking.

Dinner under the camel thorn trees

As you round the last bend in the track the camp

unfolds, a myriad of flickering lanterns hanging in the trees. The sound of laughter, friendly banter and the smell of woodsmoke fill the evening air as the tracker trains the spotlight on a few tame impala close to the lodge waterhole. Outside the camp, your muchinda welcomes you from the evening game drive and escorts you to your room to freshen up before dinner. Making your way along the narrow pathway, you hear the distant moan of a lion and the whooping call of hyenas.

After a relaxing bath, the muchinda arrives at your door to take you back to the bustling boma adorned with lanterns and candles. Upon entering, your hands are washed with rose water, an ancient Ethiopian ritual. Muchindas and hosts are all busy taking orders for drinks and passing around bowls of appetizers. More guests arrive, looking relaxed after the day's excitement. The aroma of cooking fills everyone with anticipation. A huge log fire in the center of the boma sends a fountain of sparks into the night, the leaping flames reflected in the drinks bottles and ice buckets. One of the chefs is turning and basting a large leg of lamb hanging from the branch of a tree over glowing coals. At the braais, another chef is basting shrimp kebabs with peri-peri butter and a thick column of sizzling smoke billows upward into the starry canopy.

Your ranger offers you an ice-cold gin and tonic. Everyone is discussing the day's safari and the unusual food on offer. Some guests make their way over to the braais, fascinated by all the colorful food grilling, simmering or frying on the open coals. The shrimp kebabs, on their rough hand-carved sticks, are wrapped in napkins and served straight from the fire. Meanwhile, the chef announces the menu in his deep, resonant African voice: "Tonight, we have poacher's roast — a marinated leg of lamb in mechoui, a blend of North African spices, lemon, olive oil and herbs — as well as Moroccan-style grilled baby chicken, msamba, baked butternut with rosemary, grilled sweet potatoes and, for dessert, coconut crème caramel with grenadilla."

The chefs are dextrously shaking pots and pans and adjusting the heat with shovels of coal from the blazing fire — hot work requiring speed and skill. The lamb is carved from the bone onto large wooden platters, the chickens are removed from the fire, and your muchinda offers you a delicious full-bodied cabernet to complement the meal.

Kelewele

Serves 8

Ingredients
6-8 plantains or green bananas,
  peeled
1 tbsp flour
2 tsp cayenne pepper,
  or to taste
5 tsp ground ginger
2 tsp paprika
Vegetable oil, for deep-frying
Salt

Special equipment
Deep-fryer or large, heavy-based
  saucepan

Method
1 Slice the plantains or bananas diagonally, about ⅛-inch thick.
2 Mix the flour, cayenne pepper, ginger and paprika together in a bowl.
3 Lightly dust the plantains in the flour mixture and shake off any excess.
4 In the deep-fryer or large saucepan, heat the oil to 375°F and
fry the plantains in batches until golden brown.
5 Drain on paper towels, sprinkle with salt and serve.

An appetizer or snack from Ghana, kelewele are plantains or green bananas
that have been dusted in a spicy flour mixture and deep-fried.

Kifto

Makes 12

Ingredients
½ cup Niter Kebbeh (see page 17)
1 onion, finely chopped
2 green bell peppers, finely diced
1-2 chilis, finely chopped
2 tsp grated fresh ginger
2 cloves garlic, crushed
1 tsp cardamon seeds, ground
2 tbsp freshly squeezed lemon juice
4 tsp Berbere (see page 18)
4 tsp salt
12 oz venison fillet, trimmed and
  finely diced
12 fresh paprika pods or small bell
  peppers

Method
1 Melt the niter kebbeh in a saucepan over a low heat.
2 Add the onion, bell peppers, chili, ginger, garlic and cardamon.
3 As soon as the niter kebbeh splutters, remove the saucepan from
the heat and set aside to cool.
4 Stir in the lemon juice, berbere and salt.
5 Mix in the venison, taste and adjust the seasoning as necessary.
6 Cut a small opening along the length of the paprika pods or bell peppers
and remove the seeds.
7 Spoon in the kifto and serve.

An Ethiopian version of steak tartare for which I use venison fillet, but beef
fillet would be a good alternative. I like to serve kifto stuffed into a fresh
paprika pod, however it is also delicious spooned over bruschetta made from
Spiced Ethiopian Bread (see page 122) using niter kebbeh instead of olive oil.

Briks

Makes 30

Ingredients
1 lb potatoes, peeled and diced
½ stick butter, plus ¾ stick extra, melted
1 onion, chopped
1 clove garlic, crushed
A handful of fresh parsley, chopped
¼ Preserved Lemon peel (see page 16), finely chopped (optional)
1 egg yolk
9 oz filo pastry
Salt and freshly ground pepper

Special equipment
Deep-fryer or large, heavy-based saucepan

Method
1 Cook the potatoes in boiling salted water, then drain, steam dry and mash.
2 Melt the butter in a frying pan, sauté the onion until soft, then add the garlic and cook for 1 minute.
3 Stir the onion mixture into the potato along with the parsley, lemon peel and egg yolk, then season well.
4 Cut the filo pastry into squares measuring about 4 inches across and keep them covered with a damp kitchen towel.
5 Take one square of pastry and brush it with some of the melted butter.
6 Lay another square on top at an angle and brush it with the melted butter, then repeat with another square.
7 Place a teaspoonful of the potato mixture in the center of the pastry.
8 Sit the pastry in the cup of your hand then, with your other hand, carefully pinch the ends together to enclose the potato, being careful that the bottom of the parcel does not split.
9 Place the brik on a tray lined with plastic wrap, then repeat with the remaining ingredients.
10 Heat the deep-fryer to 350°F and, working in batches, cook the briks until lightly golden.
11 Drain on paper towels and salt lightly before serving.

Tunisian street snacks, briks are crispy fried pastry parcels filled with potato, onion and a whole egg. This is a simplified version that omits the egg. Uncooked briks freeze well and can be cooked from frozen.

Kingklip and shrimp kebabs in chermoula with lemon

Serves 6

Ingredients
1½ lbs thick kingklip or halibut
   fillet
18 raw shrimp
3 lemons, quartered
Lemon leaves

For the chermoula:
1 cup olive oil
½ cup fresh lemon juice
1 onion, grated
A bunch of parsley, chopped
6 cloves garlic, crushed
1 tbsp paprika
2 tsp ground cumin
½ tsp cayenne pepper
Salt and pepper

Special equipment
6 skewers

Method
1 In a bowl, whisk together all the ingredients for the chermoula until smooth and set aside.
2 Skin the kingklip or halibut fillet and cut it into 1-inch cubes.
3 Split the shrimp down their backs and remove the dark intestinal thread.
4 Add the kingklip or halibut and shrimp to the chermoula and let them marinate for about 2 hours in the refrigerator.
5 Thread the kingklip and shrimp onto the skewers, alternating them with the lemon wedges and leaves.
6 Braai the kebabs over medium-hot coals for 8 to 10 minutes or until cooked, turning and basting with the leftover marinade from time to time; alternatively, broil them conventionally for 5 minutes.
7 Serve immediately with lemon wedges.

Peri-peri shrimp kebabs

Serves 8

Ingredients
24 raw queen or tiger shrimp
Lemon or bay leaves (optional)

For the peri-peri butter:
2 sticks butter
4 cloves garlic, crushed
½ cup olive oil
6-8 red chilis, or to taste
⅓ cup fresh lemon juice,
   or to taste
Salt

Special equipment
8 wooden skewers

Method
1 To begin the peri-peri butter, melt the butter with the garlic and set aside.
2 Heat the olive oil in a small saucepan.
3 Drop in a little of the chili to see if it skips to the surface of the oil and bubbles – if it does, it is the correct temperature.
4 Add all the chilis to the oil and immediately remove the pan from the heat, leaving the chilis to cool for 10 to 15 minutes.
5 Add the lemon juice, garlic-flavored butter and salt to the chilis.
6 To prepare the shrimp, make a small slit along the back and remove the black intestinal thread with a skewer, keeping the tail intact but removing the head if desired.
7 Thread three shrimp, facing in the same direction, onto each skewer, alternating them with the lemon or bay leaves.
8 Brush the shrimp with the peri-peri butter.
9 Braai the shrimp over hot coals, basting and turning until the shells have turned orange; alternatively, grill for 4 to 5 minutes.
10 Wrap paper napkins around the base of each skewer and hand around.

Algerian spatchcock baby chicken

Serves 6

Ingredients
2 tbsp aniseed
Juice of 3 lemons
2 onions, grated
A bunch of cilantro, chopped
2 in fresh ginger, peeled
**   and grated**
4 cloves garlic, crushed
2 tsp paprika
½ tsp cayenne pepper
A pinch of saffron threads
1 cup olive oil
3 baby chickens
Salt and pepper

Method

1 Toast the aniseed in a dry frying pan until fragrant, then crush it.
2 Combine the aniseed, lemon juice, onions, cilantro, ginger, garlic, paprika, cayenne and saffron in a bowl and whisk in the olive oil.
3 Season the marinade mixture to taste, adding more cayenne and black pepper if necessary.
4 Use a large knife to spatchcock the baby chickens, turning them breast down, inserting the knife in the body and cutting through the breast bones so the chickens can be laid flat. Trim off any excess skin or surplus fat.
5 Place the chickens in a plastic bowl and rub them with the marinade.
6 Cover and place in the fridge to marinate for a minimum of 12 hours.
7 Bring the chickens to room temperature before cooking.
8 Cook over medium-hot coals, or under a conventional broiler, turning the chicken occasionally and basting with the remaining marinade — the chicken is done when the skin is crisp and the juices run clear when the thickest part of the leg is pierced with a skewer.

Marinate the chicken for at least 12 hours, but preferably for a whole day.

Doro wat

Serves 4

Ingredients
4 chicken leg and thigh pieces
2 tbsp fresh lemon juice
2 tsp salt
3 onions, finely chopped
4 tbsp Niter Kebbeh (see page 17)
4 cloves garlic, crushed
¾ in fresh ginger, peeled
**   and grated**
¼ tsp cardamon, ground
¼ tsp fenugreek seeds, ground
A pinch of freshly ground nutmeg
4 tbsp Berbere (see page 18)
2 tbsp paprika
4 tbsp red wine
4 eggs, hard-boiled
Freshly ground pepper

Special equipment
Cast-iron casserole dish

Method

1 Pat the chicken pieces dry with the paper towels, then rub them all over with the lemon juice and salt.
2 Place the chicken in a bowl, cover with plastic wrap and let marinate for 30 minutes at room temperature.
3 Put the onions in the casserole dish without any fat and cook over a low heat, stirring constantly until they are soft and dry — you may need to take the dish off the heat from time to time if you find the onions are sticking.
4 Add the niter kebbeh and, when it starts to splutter, add one at a time the garlic, ginger, cardamon, fenugreek and nutmeg, stirring after each addition.
5 Add the berbere and paprika, stir and cook for 2 minutes.
6 Pour in the wine and ¾ cup of water, then bring to the boil, stirring.
7 Boil until the liquid reaches the consistency of heavy cream.
8 Remove the chicken from the lemon juice and pat dry.
9 Add the chicken to the simmering sauce, turning until the pieces are coated on all sides, then cover and simmer for 10 minutes.
10 Prick the hard-boiled eggs all over with a fork and add them to the chicken, gently rolling them in the sauce until coated.
11 Cover and cook for another 10 to 15 minutes or until the chicken is tender.
12 Taste the wat and adjust the seasoning as necessary before serving.

A traditional Ethiopian stew of chicken and eggs in red pepper sauce, doro wat is wrapped in Injera flat bread (see page 120) and eaten with the hands.

Moroccan-style grilled baby chicken with lemon yogurt sauce

Serves 5-10

Ingredients

5 baby chickens

For the stuffing:
½ cup raisins
1½ boiling water
3 tbsp dry white wine
2 tbsp olive oil
1 cup couscous
2 tbs butter
2 onions, chopped
2 tsp ground cinnamon
1 tsp ground cumin
½ cup flaked almonds, toasted
1 tbsp honey
1 tbsp cilantro, chopped
1 tbsp mint leaves, chopped
Salt and freshly ground pepper

For the baste:
¾ stick butter
4 tbsp honey
¾ tsp ground cinnamon
¼ tsp ground cumin

For the sauce:
¼ Preserved lemon peel (see page 16), rinsed thoroughly
1 cup plain yogurt

Method

1 To make the stuffing, cover the raisins with hot water from the tap, let soak for 30 minutes, then drain and set aside.

2 Combine the boiling water, wine and olive oil in a pitcher.

3 Place the couscous in a large bowl, pour over the wine and oil mixture, cover with a kitchen towel and let stand for 15 to 20 minutes.

4 Season the couscous and separate the grains with a fork.

5 Melt the butter in a frying pan and sauté the onions until soft and translucent.

6 Add the cinnamon and cumin and cook for 2 to 3 minutes.

7 Stir the onion mixture, flaked almonds, honey, cilantro and mint into the couscous, then season to taste and set aside.

8 Melt all the baste ingredients together in a saucepan and season to taste.

9 To make the sauce, finely chop the preserved lemon peel, stir it into the yogurt and add black pepper to taste.

10 Remove any innards from the chickens and trim off any surplus fat from inside the cavity, then divide the stuffing equally among the cavities.

11 Tie the legs together with kitchen string, brush each bird with the baste and wrap in a double layer of buttered foil.

12 Place over medium-slow burning coals and cook for 45 to 60 minutes, turning turn every 3 to 5 minutes, until cooked — the juices should run clear when the thickest part of the thigh is pierced with a skewer.

13 Unwrap the chickens, baste them with the remaining mixture and cook on the grate over medium coals to crisp up the skin.

14 Serve the chickens with the lemon yogurt sauce in a separate bowl.

The stuffed chickens can also be roasted in a moderate oven, basting frequently, for around 45 minutes or until they are cooked.

Jeanette's bobotie

Serves 8

Ingredients
2 onions, chopped
3 tbsp sunflower oil
2 tbsp paprika
2 tbsp turmeric
2 tsp hot curry powder
2 tsp ground ginger
1 tsp cayenne pepper
2 tsp sugar
2 tsp salt
1¾ cup/14 oz canned chopped
   tomatoes
½ cup raisins
4 oz tomato paste
4 tbsp fruit chutney
2 tbsp red wine vinegar
2 tbsp Worcestershire sauce
2 tbsp apricot jam
3 slices bread, crusts removed,
   and cubed
1 cup milk
4lb 8 oz ground beef or venison
2 eggs, beaten
A few lemon leaves or bay leaves

Method
1 Sauté the onions in the sunflower oil until soft and translucent.
2 Add all the spices, sugar and salt and cook for 2 to 3 minutes.
3 Remove from the heat and add the tomatoes, raisins, tomato paste, chutney, vinegar, Worcestershire sauce and jam.
4 Return to the heat, bring to a boil and gently simmer for 2 to 3 minutes.
5 Meanwhile, soak the bread cubes in a little of the milk.
6 Add the ground meat to the onion and tomato mixture and mix thoroughly.
7 Squeeze dry the bread, reserving the milk, and add the bread to the ground meat.
8 Cook the mixture for 45 to 60 minutes, stirring occasionally, until the excess liquid has evaporated.
9 Meanwhile, preheat the oven to 350°F.
10 Adjust the seasoning of the meat mixture as necessary, then transfer it to an ovenproof dish.
11 In a bowl, beat together the eggs and all the milk, then pour over the meat mixture.
12 Decorate the surface of the custard with the lemon or bay leaves and bake in the oven for about 15 to 20 minutes, or until the custard is set.

A recipe originating from the Cape Malay people, this curried ground meat and dried fruit mixture is topped with a baked custard that has been spiked with lemon leaves or fresh bay leaves. It is traditionally served with yellow rice.

Guinea fowl in harissa

Serves 6

Ingredients
6 guinea fowl
3½ cups Harissa (see page 16)

Method
1 Spatchcock each guinea fowl by turning them breast down, inserting a knife in the body cavities and cutting through the breastbones.
2 Open out the guinea fowl, placing them skin-side up, and with the palm of your hand gently press onto the backbones to flatten the birds.
3 Trim off any surplus skin and fat.
4 Place the guinea fowl in a large plastic container, pour in the harissa and rub it thoroughly into the birds.
5 Cover and place in the refrigerator to marinate for at least 12 hours, and preferably for 24 hours.
6 Remove the guinea fowl from the marinade and grill over medium-slow burning coals; alternatively, cook in an oven set to 350°F for 20 to 30 minutes or until done, then place the guinea fowl under a broiler to crisp up the skin if necessary.

Harissa also makes a delicious marinade for grilled or roast chicken or lamb. Serve them with piquant Mint Chutney (see page 18).

A poacher's roast by the light of the silvery moon

Special equipment
Suitable tree
Wooden prop
Rope
Shovel
Survival knife
Pile of dry wood
Dry grass
Matches
Catch tray (optional)
Leg of lamb or venison
Skewer

Method

1 Find a tree with a branch that bows out and is within arm's reach, ensuring it is also free of any snakes, bees, leopards etc.

2 Build and light a campfire nearby — caution: excess smoke could alert the authorities.

3 Carve a wooden prop from a stick — this will be needed later to rest the leg on its side during cooking.

4 Lasso the rope around the branch, ensuring the rope is long enough to tie the meat close to the ground.

5 Attach the meat to the rope by knotting it through the hock.

6 Place a catch tray on the ground in case there is a problem with your knots!

7 Balance the leg on its side with the wooden prop.

8 Using the shovel, place fresh coals from the fire under the meat.

9 Roast for 20 minutes, then turn the leg and cook on the other side, placing additional fresh coals from the fire under the meat from time to time.

10 Remove the prop and allow the meat to hang from the tree branch, roasting for a further 20 minutes.

11 To test if the meat is cooked, use a skewer to pierce the meat at its thickest part and check the ease with which the skewer goes in.

12 For poachers in a hurry, the cooked outer meat can be carved off while the rest of the leg continues to roast.

13 Slip away undetected.

Poacher's roasts should be attempted only with the assistance of an experienced poacher and on nights when the moon is full.

Lamb in mechoui

Serves 8

Ingredients
6¾ lbs leg of lamb with knuckle

For the mechoui:
20 mint leaves, chopped
4 tbsp freshly squeezed lemon juice
4 tbsp olive oil
2 cloves garlic, crushed
2 tbsp ground coriander
2 tsp ground cumin
2 tsp paprika
1 tsp cayenne pepper
Salt

Method

1 Prepare the mechoui by mixing all the ingredients together in a bowl.

2 Rub the marinade over the leg of lamb.

3 Place the meat in a plastic container and let marinate for 24 hours in the refrigerator or other very cool place.

4 Preheat the oven to 350°F, or prepare your tree and fire.

5 Sprinkle the lamb with salt and roast for 15 to 17 minutes per pound.

If you wish to cook this recipe in the style of a poacher's roast, please find your location the day before and make sure you will have help. Check the weather forecast too!

Fritz Rabe's family recipe for puffadder

Serves 8-16

Ingredients
1 large sheep intestine
2¼ lb ox liver, thinly sliced
2 ox kidneys
3½ oz sheep or pork fat
2 onions, finely chopped
4-6 cloves garlic, crushed
1 tbsp salt
1 tbsp freshly ground pepper
2 tsp coriander seeds, ground

Special equipment
Kitchen string
Plastic funnel or plastic bottle with
  base removed

Method

1 Turn the intestine inside out and place the opening over a tap, holding it firmly in place with your hand.
2 Turn on the tap and wash the intestine thoroughly, checking that there are no holes in the skin.
3 Leave the intestine to soak in fresh water until ready to use.
4 Remove the membrane from the liver, then dice liver and place in a bowl.
5 To prepare the kidneys, remove the outer membrane, cut in half horizontally and, with a sharp pair of scissors, remove the core.
6 Dice the kidneys the same size as the liver and add to the bowl.
7 Chop the sheep fat the same size as the liver and add it to the bowl.
8 Stir in the onions, garlic and seasonings and mix until combined.
9 Lift one end of the intestine out of the water and remove the excess water by carefully sliding your hand down the length of the skin.
10 Secure the end with kitchen string.
11 Place the funnel or bottle neck into the other end of the intestine and hold it up so the remaining casing falls back into the water.
12 With your other hand, spoon a little of the filling into the funnel and push it down with the end of a wooden spoon.
13 Gently ease the filling down the casing with your hand, keeping the casing wet and being careful not to split it.
14 Continue with the remaining filling until it looks like a puffadder — be careful not to over-fill the intestine as it may split when cooking.
15 Fasten the open end of the sausage with string.
16 Keep the puffadder covered in water and refrigerate until ready to cook.
17 Loosely coil the puffadder onto a braai grate over gentle coals and cook for about 1 hour, turning once halfway through — when cooked, it will be firm to touch and dark brown in color; alternatively, the puffadder can be broiled.
18 Cut into portions and enjoy.

Fritz Rabe grew up in the Kruger National Park. His family has been game farming for decades and his grandfather, Buks Venter, was an elephant control officer for Botswana, Rhodesia (Zimbabwe) and South Africa. Fritz describes himself as a second generation vegetarian because the cows eat grass and he eats the cows. Game intestine, liver and kidney are traditionally used for this recipe, but it is just as delicious when ox is used. The freshness of the ingredients is important and the intestine must be stored in cold water until you are ready to make the puffadder. It takes time to prepare but is well worth the effort and can be made the day before eating. The secret is to cook the puffadder slowly over a low heat. Fritz suggests eating this with Mealiepap (see page 119) and tomato sauce or rice and a salad.

Fritz Rabe's skilpadjies

Serves 10

Ingredients
10 pieces caul fat
5oz rump steak
2¼ lbs ox liver, thinly sliced
2 ox kidneys
3½ oz sheep fat
2 onions, finely chopped
4-6 cloves garlic, crushed
1 tbsp salt
1 tbsp freshly ground pepper

Special equipment
Toothpicks

Method
1 Cover the caul fat with water until ready to use.
2 Prepare the filling in the same way as for the puffadder (opposite), cutting the rump steak into similarly sized cubes to the liver, kidney and sheep fat.
3 Add the onions, garlic, salt and pepper and mix well.
4 Take a piece of caul fat and gently lay it out flat, checking to see that there are no tears in the lattice.
5 Drape the caul fat over your hand and place a large spoonful of the meat mixture into the cup of your hand.
6 With your other hand, gently fold over the caul fat, encasing the mixture.
7 Secure the ends with a couple of toothpicks, then place the skilpadjie on a tray lined with plastic wrap and cover.
8 Repeat until all the mixture is used.
9 Place the skilpadjies on a braai grate over gentle coals and cook them slowly for 30 to 45 minutes, turning over halfway through cooking; alternatively, cook them slowly in an oven set to 275°F.

Skilpadjie is the Afrikaans word for tortoise. The mixture is very similar to a puffadder but with the addition of steak. It is wrapped in caul fat and, once cooked, looks similar to a tortoise shell. Fresh ingredients are important but it can be prepared the day before. This recipe is best made with venison steak and cooked slowly over coals. If the skilpadjies are drying out before they are fully cooked, cover them with foil.

Marinated venison kebabs

Makes 8-10

Ingredients
1¼ lbs venison, cubed
10 shallots
1 red bell pepper
1 yellow bell pepper
1 green bell pepper

For the marinade:
1 cup olive oil
1 onion, grated
2 cloves garlic, crushed
1 tsp thyme
½ cup soy sauce
2 tbsp red wine vinegar
4½ tsp salt
1 tsp English mustard powder
A small bunch of basil leaves,
 chopped

Special equipment
8-10 skewers

Method
1 Mix all the marinade ingredients together in a non-corrosive dish
and marinate the venison for 4 to 10 days in the refrigerator.
2 When ready to assemble the kebabs, blanch the shallots in boiling
water for 5 minutes, then refresh under cold running water.
3 Cut the bell peppers into large pieces.
4 Thread the venison cubes on the skewers, alternating them with
the pieces of bell pepper and the shallots.
5 Braai the kebabs over hot coals or broil them conventionally,
turning occasionally until the meat is cooked medium to medium-rare.

For this recipe, choose a loin or leg cut of venison and marinate
the meat for at least 4 days, longer if you can.

Orange-scented oxtail

Serves 6

Ingredients
¾ cup flour
½ tsp English mustard powder
½ tsp ground coriander
½ tsp ground cumin
1½ tsp dried thyme
4½ lbs oxtail, trimmed and
 cut into 2½ in pieces
¼ cup oil
2 onions, sliced
2 stalks celery, sliced
4 cloves garlic, sliced
1½ cup dry white wine
3¼ cups quality beef stock
1¾ cups/14 oz canned chopped
 tomatoes
Pared zest of 1 orange
6 parsley stalks
1 tsp dried basil
1 bay leaf
Lemon juice, to taste
Dijon mustard, to taste
Salt and pepper

Special equipment
Ovenproof casserole
Food processor or blender

Method
1 Mix together the flour, mustard powder, coriander, cumin and ½ teaspoon
of the dried thyme.
2 Lightly dredge the oxtail with the seasoned flour.
3 Heat the oil in a frying pan and brown the oxtail in batches, transferring
each batch to a casserole dish.
4 Deglaze the frying pan with some of the wine and add it to the casserole.
5 In the same pan, sweat the onions, celery and garlic until soft.
6 Pour the remaining wine into the frying pan and boil until reduced by half.
7 Add the onion mixture to the casserole with the stock, tomatoes, orange
zest, parsley stalks, dried basil, bay leaf and 1 teaspoon of dried thyme.
8 If the meat is not yet covered, add water as necessary, then bring the
casserole to a boil on the stovetop.
9 Transfer the casserole to an oven set to 275°F and cook for 3 to 4 hours
or until the meat is very tender and pulls easily from the bone.
10 Strain off the liquid from the casserole and discard the parsley stalks,
orange zest and bay leaf.
11 Set the meat aside in a warm place until ready to serve.
12 Liquidize the sauce, then adjust the seasoning to taste, adding lemon
juice, Dijon mustard and salt and pepper as necessary.
13 Reheat the sauce before serving it with the oxtail.

Ostrich neck makes a good substitute for oxtail. There is very little difference
in taste — the only giveaway is the shape of the bones.

As the day cools down, the rhythm picks up

TOP ROW LEFT TO RIGHT: A warm reception awaits your return to Macatoo Camp; a muchinda lights the boma lanterns before dark; Jan really loved photographing those Ilala palm trees!
BOTTOM ROW LEFT TO RIGHT: As the sun sets, the cheetah, the fastest mammal in the world, has a final attempt at an impala in the long grass; in Africa, singing and dancing are spontaneous.

Rice pilaf

Serves 4-6

Ingredients
2 tbsp olive oil
2 onions, finely chopped
1¾ cups basmati rice
½ cup raisins
1 chili, chopped, or to taste
4 tsp grated lime zest
1-2 sticks cinnamon
Seeds of 2 cardamon pods, crushed
2 tsp salt
½ cup slivered almonds
4 tbsp parsley leaves, chopped
Freshly ground pepper

Method
1 In a large saucepan, heat the oil and sauté the onions until soft.
2 Stir in the rice and cook, stirring frequently, for 4 minutes.
3 Add the raisins, chili, lime zest, cinnamon sticks, cardamon,
salt and 4 cups of water and stir well.
4 Cover the pan and simmer for 15 to 18 minutes or until the rice
has absorbed all the liquid.
5 Meanwhile, lightly toast the slivered almonds in a dry frying pan.
6 Remove the saucepan from the heat and fluff up the rice with a fork.
7 Stir in the almonds, parsley and season to taste before serving.

Mealiepap

Serves 6

Ingredients
3 tbsp olive oil
2 tsp rosemary or thyme
1-2 tsp salt
2 cups coarse mealie or corn meal

Method

1 Bring 4 cups of water to the boil in a heavy-based pot.

2 Add the olive oil, rosemary or thyme and salt to the boiling water, letting it return to a boil if necessary.

3 Add all the mealie or corn meal at once, stirring constantly until the meal and water are thoroughly combined.

4 Cover, reduce the heat and simmer for 40 minutes, stirring occasionally.

5 Add ½ cup of cold water to the mixture and continue simmering for a further 30 minutes before serving.

This is the staple dish of Africa, although different countries and areas have different names for it. Like all African meals, it is eaten by hand. First the hands are dipped in water, then a small ball of the mixture is rolled around several times before being dipped in a sauce or stew and eaten. The mixture tastes bland; I prefer the coarse ground variety and cook it with olive oil and herbs. Mealiepap can be cooked to the consistency of oatmeal and eaten in the morning with milk and sugar. When cooked to a drier consistency, it is known as stywe or putu and generally eaten with meat or a gravy. A crumbly version, called krummelpap in South Africa, is made as above but using 2¼ cups of water and 3¼ cups of mealie meal. Krummelpap also needs to be stirred more frequently than mealiepap, to ensure the mixture is crumbly but free from lumps. Making mealiepap in large quantities gives your upper body a good workout! A simple way to serve it is with a tomato and onion sauce, to which you can add a little chili if desired.

Couscous with caramelized onions and raisins

Serves 8

Ingredients
4 eggs
¾ cup almonds
1 onion, chopped
¾ stick butter
⅔ cup raisins
2½ tbsp brown sugar
1 tbsp grated fresh ginger
2 tsp ground cinnamon
4 cups chicken stock
A pinch of saffron threads
2¾ cups couscous
A few sprigs of mint, chopped
Salt and pepper

Method

1 Hard boil the eggs, then peel and chop them.

2 Meanwhile, toast the almonds in a dry frying pan until golden, then chop.

3 In a saucepan sweat the onion with three-quarters of the butter until soft.

4 Add the raisins, sugar, ginger and cinnamon and continue to cook, stirring occasionally until the mixture caramelizes.

5 Set the onion mixture aside in a warm place.

6 Place the chicken stock in a saucepan with the saffron and bring to the boil.

7 In a large bowl, pour the stock over the couscous, add the remaining butter, then cover and let stand for 10 minutes.

8 Fluff up the couscous with a fork and stir in the eggs, almonds and mint.

9 Season to taste and serve topped with the caramelized onion mixture.

Stick bread

Method

1 Put the beer, butter and sugar into a saucepan, bring to a boil then remove from the heat and set aside to cool until lukewarm.

2 Add the beaten eggs.

3 Place the flours, yeast and salt in the bowl of the electric mixer and make a well in the center.

4 Pour in the beer and egg mixture and mix to form a soft dough.

5 Knead the dough until smooth and elastic.

6 Place the dough in a greased bowl, loosely cover with some greased plastic wrap or a shower cap, and place in a warm, draft-free place until the dough has doubled in size, about 1 hour.

7 Knock back the dough.

8 This is the fun part: divide the dough into 8 pieces and roll each piece into the shape of a snake.

9 Wrap the dough along the length of the sticks, leaving ample space at the end for holding the sticks over the fire.

10 Hold the dough over slow-burning coals and turn occasionally until the bread is cooked and browned, about 7 to 12 minutes depending on the heat of the coals — the dough will slide off the stick easily when cooked.

Here is an excellent campfire bread that is great for children, providing you are careful to protect their hands. A knob of garlic butter or a spoonful of apricot jam placed in the hollow of the bread are delicious ways to eat it.

Makes 8

Ingredients
1¼ cups beer
½ stick butter
4 tsp brown sugar
1 egg, beaten
2 cups white bread flour
2 cups whole wheat flour
1 envelope instant dried yeast
1 tsp salt

Special equipment
Electric mixer with dough hook
Long sticks

Injera

Makes 6-8

Ingredients
5 cups self-rising flour
1¼ cups whole wheat flour
1 tsp baking powder
2 tsp salt
18 floz soda water
Vegetable oil, for frying

Method

1 Combine all the dry ingredients in a large bowl and make a well in the center.

2 Gradually beat in the soda water and 4 cups of plain water until a smooth, thin batter is obtained.

3 Heat a crêpe pan until hot.

4 Add a little oil and swirl it around the pan.

5 Pour in some batter, swirling it around to form a thin layer like a crêpe.

6 Cook the bread until bubbles appear on the surface, then flip over and cook the other side for 2 or 3 minutes.

7 Place the cooked injera on a plate, cover with a kitchen towel to keep warm and continue until all the batter is used.

Roosterkoek and Ashkoek

Makes 10-12

Ingredients
2½ cups bread flour
1 envelope instant dried yeast
2 tsp sugar
1½ tsp salt
½-¾ cup buttermilk
4 tbsp lukewarm water
1½ tbsp butter, melted

Special equipment
Electric mixer with dough hook
Long handled tongs

Method
1 Place the flour, yeast, sugar and salt into the bowl of an electric mixer and make a well in the center.
2 Add the buttermilk, water and melted butter and mix to form a soft dough.
3 Knead until smooth and elastic.
4 Place the dough in a greased bowl and lightly cover with a sheet of greased plastic wrap or a shower cap.
5 Let stand in a warm, draft-free place until the dough has doubled in size, about 1 hour.
6 Meanwhile, light your fire and allow it to burn down to slow-burning coals for roosterkoek, or to smoldering ash for the ashkoek.
7 With floured hands, pull off some dough, roll it into a ball, then flatten into a disk using the edge of your hand in a rocking motion.
8 Place the dough on the heated grate, or in the ash using the long handled tongs — the bread will puff up as soon as it starts to cook.
9 Turn the bread over as soon as it starts to color and cook the other side until it sounds hollow when tapped — if the bread is coloring too quickly without cooking properly, allow your fire to burn down longer.
10 Remove from the heat, tap off the ash and enjoy.

Roosterkoek is a bread cooked on a braai grate over slow-burning coals while ashkoek is cooked in the smoldering embers of the fire. The recipe here is for a buttermilk bread but most doughs are suited to these cooking methods.

Spiced Ethiopian bread

Makes 1 loaf

Ingredients
½ cup Niter Kebbeh (see
    page 17), melted
2½ cups lukewarm water
2 tbsp ground coriander
2 tsp salt
1 tsp ground cardamon
1 tsp ground fenugreek seeds
½ tsp finely ground pepper
6-6½ cups flour
2 envelopes instant dried yeast
½ tsp Berbere (see page 18)

Special equipment
Electric mixer with dough hook

Method
1 Mix two-thirds of the niter kibbeh with the water, spices and salt.
2 Place 6 cups of the flour in the bowl of an electric mixer
and sprinkle in the dried yeast.
3 Make a well in the center and pour in the spiced butter liquid.
4 Work together until the mixture forms a soft dough — if it is too sticky,
add a little more flour.
5 Knead the dough until smooth and elastic.
6 Cut off a piece of dough about the size of a bread roll.
7 Shape the remaining dough into a round flattened loaf and place
on a large ungreased baking sheet.
8 Using a sharp knife, score the loaf into quarters or eighths.
9 Make a little indentation on the top of the loaf with your thumb.
10 Shape the remaining dough into a small flattened ball and firmly place
it on top of the loaf where you have made the indentation.
11 Cover the dough with greased plastic wrap or a shower cap and place
in a warm, draft-free place until it doubles in size, approximately 1 hour.
12 Preheat the oven to 350°F and bake the loaf in the middle of the oven for
50 to 60 minutes until crusty and golden brown.
13 Place on a cooling rack and, while warm, combine the remaining niter
kibbeh with the berbere and brush evenly over the top as a glaze.

Baked baby potatoes with ras el hanout

Serves 8

Ingredients
4½ lbs baby potatoes
6 tbsp olive oil
3 tbsp Ras el Hanout (see page 17)
Salt
Lemon wedges (optional)

Method
1 Preheat the oven to 350°F.
2 Place the potatoes in a roasting pan and rub them with the olive oil.
3 Sprinkle the ras el hanout over the potatoes, rolling them around several times until they are evenly coated.
4 Roast in the oven for 30 to 40 minutes or until cooked through.
5 Sprinkle with salt before serving with the lemon wedges.

Grilled sweet potatoes with rosemary garlic butter

Serves 8

Ingredients
4 sweet potatoes
1 stick butter
1 clove garlic, chopped
A squeeze of fresh lemon juice
2-4 sprigs fresh rosemary, finely chopped
Freshly ground black pepper

Method
1 Preheat the oven to 350°F.
2 Bake the sweet potatoes until they are three-quarters cooked — they will still feel hard in the center when pressed.
3 Meanwhile, melt the butter in a saucepan, add the garlic, lemon juice, rosemary and pepper to taste and set aside.
4 When the potatoes are ready, cut them in half horizontally.
5 Using a sharp knife, cut hatch marks into the flesh without going all the way through to the skin.
6 Brush the surfaces of the sweet potatoes with the flavored butter.
7 Braai or broil the sweet potatoes cut-side down on a grate over medium-hot coals until the grate has charred its pattern onto the potato.
8 Turn the sweet potatoes over, baste them with the flavored butter and continue cooking on the other side.
9 Sprinkle the sweet potatoes with salt before serving.

The sweet potatoes are first baked, then grilled over coals to finish. This recipe can also be cooked using a ridged cast-iron pan.

Ethiopian mash with niter kebbeh

Serves 8

Ingredients
3 lbs potatoes
1 cup Niter Kebbeh (see page 17)
1½-2¼ cups milk
Salt and pepper

Method
1 Peel the potatoes and cook in boiling salted water until tender.
2 Drain the potatoes, then allow to steam dry.
3 Meanwhile, in separate saucepans, melt the niter kebbeh and heat the milk.
4 Mash the potatoes with the melted niter kebbeh, adding the hot milk to give the desired consistency.
5 Season to taste and serve hot.

Carrot purée with ras el hanout

Serves 6

Ingredients
½ stick butter
**2¼ lbs carrots, peeled and
thinly sliced**
2 tbsp Ras el Hanout (see page 17)
½ cup cream
Salt

Special equipment
Food processor or liquidizer

Method

1 Melt the butter in a pan, add the carrots, cover and cook slowly, stirring from time to time and adding a little water if necessary to prevent burning.
2 When the carrots are nearly tender, add the ras el hanout and cook for another 2 to 3 minutes.
3 Remove the carrots from the heat, transfer them to a food processor and purée until smooth.
4 Add the cream and salt to taste, then reheat the mixture before serving.

Braaied mealies with herb butter

Serves 6

Ingredients
**6 mealies or corn on the cob,
preferably with husks**

For the herb butter:
5 tbsp butter, softened
Fresh thyme
Pepper
Fresh lemon juice
1 clove garlic, chopped (optional)

Method

1 To make the herb butter, mix all the ingredients together, adding the flavorings to taste and set aside.
2 To prepare the corn, carefully peel back the husks and remove the silks.
3 Place in a pot of boiling, salted water and cook for 5 minutes.
4 Drain, then refresh under cold water and dry well.
5 Brush the corn with the herb butter then carefully fold the husks back over to enclose the corn.
6 Place on a grate over slow-burning coals, turning occasionally.
7 When the husks are charred, pull them back, twisting them together to form a handle, and serve.

Baked butternut with rosemary

Serves 8

Ingredients
2 butternut squash
4 tbsp olive oil
8 sprigs rosemary
Salt and freshly ground pepper

Method

1 Preheat the oven to 350°F.
2 Cut the butternuts in half and use a spoon to scoop out the seeds.
3 Cut each half in half and rub with the olive oil.
4 Diagonally thread a sprig of rosemary through each piece of squash, pushing a skewer through the butternut first to make it easier.
5 Place in a roasting pan and season with salt and pepper.
6 Bake for about 30 minutes or until the butternut is tender when pierced with a small sharp knife.

Gem squash stuffed with potato, leek and dates

Serves 8

Ingredients
5 gem, buttercup, or acorn squash, halved
2 potatoes, peeled and cubed
½ stick butter, plus extra for greasing
4 leeks, thinly sliced
1 clove garlic
2 tbsp dried dates, chopped
½ cup parmesan cheese, grated
Salt and pepper

Method
1 Cook the squash in boiling salted water until they are tender, then drain and set aside to cool.
2 Meanwhile, cook the potatoes in a separate pan of boiling salted water until tender, then drain and mash them.
3 Melt the butter in a frying pan and sauté the leeks and garlic until soft.
4 Remove the pan from the heat and add the mashed potato and the flesh of the squash, reserving the shells.
5 Stir in the dates and season the mixture to taste.
6 Spoon the filling into the reserved squash shells (there should be sufficient filling for at least 8 shells) and sprinkle with parmesan.
7 Loosely wrap the filled squash in buttered foil and reheat thoroughly for 10 to 15 minutes in an oven set to 300°F; alternatively, place the squash over slow burning coals until the filling is hot.
8 Remove the foil and serve.

Msamba

Serves 6-8

Ingredients
⅔ cup raw unsalted peanuts
2¾ lb young pumpkin leaves,
  washed
4 tbsp olive oil
2 onions, finely chopped
6 tomatoes, chopped
Salt and freshly ground pepper

Special equipment
Mortar and pestle

Method
1 Grind the peanuts to a fine powder and set aside.
2 Roll the pumpkin leaves together into a roll and chop.
3 Heat the oil in a large saucepan or pot and sauté the onions
until they are soft and translucent.
4 Add the chopped tomatoes and cook until they are soft
and the juices have evaporated.
5 Add the pumpkin leaves, stirring until they are wilted
and tender — the mixture should not be watery.
6 Mix in the ground peanuts and season to taste before serving.

One of my favorite vegetable dishes, this recipe comes from Malawi.
It can be made with the leaves of young pumpkin or sweet potato
or, if these are not available, with kale or spinach.

Zulu cabbage

Serves 6-8

Ingredients
1 small white cabbage
1 onion
1 green bell pepper
2-3 tbsp sunflower oil
1½ cups/12 oz canned tomatoes, chopped with juice reserved
1 tbsp mild curry powder
Salt and pepper

Method

1 Slice or chop the cabbage, onion and bell pepper as preferred.

2 Heat the oil in a frying pan and sauté the onion and bell pepper until they are soft and the onion is translucent.

3 Add the cabbage, cover and cook until it begins to wilt.

4 Add all the remaining ingredients and cook for about 30 minutes, stirring occasionally and adding a little water if necessary to prevent sticking.

5 Taste and adjust the seasoning as necessary before serving hot.

A Zulu chef named Musa gave me this recipe when I was working in Kwa-Zulu Natal. He recommended that it be served with Mealiepap (see page 119). There are similar versions of this dish made in Ethiopia and Kenya.

With sunsets like this, who needs the cinema

TOP ROW LEFT TO RIGHT:
Evening skies over the
Zambezi River, just up from
Victoria Falls; a traditional
ebony figurine — as ebony
is rare these curios now
tend to be made from soft
woods; pinks and mauves
feature at the beginning of
sunset; as the sun touches
the horizon, deep reds and
oranges predominate.
BOTTOM ROW LEFT TO
RIGHT: The more clouds
there are in the sky, the
more spectacular the
sunset; time to reflect
on the day's events over
a gin and tonic at a bush
bar in the Delta.

Coconut crème caramel with grenadilla

Serves 8

Ingredients
8 grenadilla or passionfruit, halved

For the caramel:
¾ cup white sugar
3 tbsp boiling water

For the custard:
4 eggs plus 2 egg yolks
¾ cup white sugar
3 cups coconut milk
1 cup cream
½ cup flaked coconut
1 tsp vanilla extract

Special equipment
8 ramekins or dariole moulds
Roasting pan

Method

1 To make the caramel, combine the white sugar in a small saucepan with 1 tablespoon of cold water.

2 Place over a low heat and stir constantly until the sugar turns to caramel.

3 Remove the pan from the heat and carefully stir in the boiling water.

4 Pour the caramel into the ramekins and set aside.

5 To make the custard, preheat the oven to 250°F.

6 In a large bowl, beat together the eggs, yolks and sugar until combined.

7 Place the coconut milk, cream and flaked coconut in a large saucepan and bring the mixture to the boil.

8 Slowly whisk the hot coconut milk mixture into the eggs, then strain.

9 Pour the custard into the ramekins and let sit for a few minutes.

10 Top up the ramekins if necessary, then stand them in a roasting pan and half-fill the pan with hot water.

11 Bake the custards for about 45 minutes — they should be set on the outside but wobble in the middle when gently shaken.

12 Remove the ramekins from the pan and leave to stand on a cooling rack.

13 Place the cooled custards in the refrigerator to chill.

14 When ready to serve, use your fingers to ease around the edge of the ramekins, shaking them gently until the custards pull away from the sides.

15 Unmold onto a plate, spoon some grenadilla or passionfruit around the crème caramels and serve.

Watermelon, mint and vodka sorbet

Serves 6-8

Ingredients
1 cup superfine sugar
2 sprigs peppermint
1¾ lbs watermelon, diced
3 tbsp vodka
1 tbsp fresh lemon juice

Special equipment
Food processor
Ice-cream machine

Method

1 Place the sugar in a saucepan with 1 cup of water and bring to a boil, stirring to dissolve the sugar.

2 Add the sprigs of peppermint, allow to cool, then chill.

3 Purée the watermelon and pass it through a strainer to remove any seeds.

4 Remove the peppermint from the syrup, then add syrup to the watermelon and purée with the vodka and lemon juice.

5 Place the mixture in an ice-cream machine and churn until frozen.

This stunning pink sorbet is best made and eaten the same day.
Don't get carried away adding more vodka or the sorbet won't freeze.
You could use Chili Vodka (see page 36) for an extra kick.

Tanzanian pineapple salad

Serves 8

Ingredients
3 large pineapples
⅔ cup cashew nuts
½ cup coconut slivers
1 cup cream
4 tbsp honey
1-2 shots white rum, or to taste

Method
1 Peel the pineapples and cut the flesh into cubes.
2 In a dry frying pan, toast separately the cashews and coconut until lightly browned, then set aside to cool.
3 Mix together the cream, honey and rum to taste and pour this mixture over the pineapple cubes.
4 Reserve some of the toasted cashews and coconut to use as a garnish, then add the remainder to the pineapple.
5 Mix well and place in the refrigerator to chill.
6 Before serving, garnish with the reserved cashews and coconut slivers.

Melktert

Serves 12

Ingredients

For the crust:
9 tbsp butter
2 tbsp sugar
1 egg
1⅓ cup flour
1 tsp baking powder
½ tsp vanilla extract

For the filling:
⅓ cup flour
5 tbsp cornstarch
2 tbsp custard powder
5 cups milk
⅔ cup white sugar
2 eggs, separated
1 vanilla bean, split in half
2 tsp butter
1 tsp baking powder
2 tsp superfine sugar
2 tsp ground cinnamon

Special equipment
11 in fluted tart tin
Baking beans

Method
1 To make the crust, beat the butter and sugar together until light and creamy.
2 Add the egg, flour, baking powder and vanilla and mix until combined.
3 Press the pastry into the tart tin and chill for 45 minutes.
4 Preheat the oven to 350°F.
5 Lay a sheet of wax paper or foil inside the pastry case so that the edges come over the rim and fill with the baking beans.
6 Bake the pastry case for 15 minutes or until the sides begin to color.
7 Remove the baking beans and paper or foil and continue cooking the pastry case for 5 minutes to dry out the base.
8 To make the filling, mix together the flour and cornstarch, adding a little of the milk to form a smooth paste.
9 Place the remaining milk in a saucepan with the sugar, egg yolks, vanilla bean and the cornstarch paste.
10 Bring to a boil, stirring continuously, and simmer for 3 minutes.
11 Remove from the heat, stir in the butter and baking powder and set aside.
12 Whisk the egg whites until they form soft peaks.
13 Fold the whites into the custard mixture, then spoon into the pastry case, discarding the vanilla bean.
14 In a small bowl, stir together the superfine sugar and cinnamon; then sprinkle the mixture over the custard filling.
15 Place the tart in the refrigerator and allow to set.

Pumpkin bread pudding

Serves 6-8

Ingredients

For the pumpkin bread:
¼ cup pecan nuts
1¼ cup pumpkin purée
2 eggs, beaten
½ cup oil
⅓ cup milk
2 cups flour
¾ cup sugar
1 tsp baking soda
¾ tsp ground cinnamon
¾ tsp ground nutmeg
½ tsp ground cloves
½ tsp ground ginger
½ tsp salt

For the pumpkin custard:
1 cup milk
1 cup cream
⅓ cup sugar
5 large egg yolks
3oz pumpkin purée
1 tsp vanilla extract
¼ tsp ground cinnamon
¼ tsp ground ginger
¼ tsp ground nutmeg

Special equipment
2lb 4oz loaf pan, greased
6-8 ramekins, greased

Method

1 To begin the pumpkin bread, preheat the oven to 350°F.

2 Lightly roast the pecans in the oven, then allow to cool and coarsely chop.

3 In a large bowl, mix together the pumpkin purée and the eggs.

4 Add the oil and milk and mix well.

5 Sift together the flour, sugar, baking soda, spices and salt.

6 Stir the sifted dry ingredients and pecans into the pumpkin mixture.

7 Spoon into the greased loaf pan and bake for 50 to 60 minutes or until a skewer inserted in the middle comes out clean.

8 Remove the loaf from the pan and place on a wire rack to cool.

9 The next day, thickly slice the bread, cut into 1-inch cubes and lightly toast them under a broiler.

10 Preheat the oven to 275°F.

11 To make the custard, place the milk, cream and 2 tablespoons of the sugar in a saucepan, bring to the boil and remove from the heat.

12 Place the egg yolks, pumpkin purée, vanilla extract, spices and the remaining sugar in a bowl and whisk together.

13 Slowly pour the hot milk onto the egg mixture and whisk until combined.

14 Divide the pumpkin bread cubes among the ramekins, filling to the top.

15 Stand the ramekins in a roasting pan, pour the custard over the bread and allow to soak for 10 to 15 minutes.

16 Top up the ramekins with more custard, if necessary.

17 Half-fill the roasting pan with hot water then place it in the oven for approximately 30 minutes or until the custard is set.

It is best to make the pumpkin bread the day before; there will be some left over but it can be frozen to eat on another occasion.

Spiked fruit with star anise syrup

Serves 8

Ingredients
3½ lbs mixed fruit, such as
  blueberries, cherries,
  strawberries, papaya and
  pineapple
Lightly whipped cream, to serve

For the syrup:
1¾ cups white sugar
1¼ cup star anise

Method

1 To make the syrup, place the sugar and star anise in a saucepan with 3¼ cups of water.

2 Bring to a boil, cooking for 7 to 10 minutes, until syrupy.

3 Let the syrup cool.

4 Cut the fruit into equally-sized pieces.

5 Strain the syrup to remove the star anise, then return the syrup to the saucepan and add the fruit.

6 Place over a moderate heat and poach the fruits in the syrup until warmed through.

7 Serve the fruit in bowls with lots of syrup and some whipped cream.

The syrup can be made well in advance and kept in the fridge until needed. This is a great dessert to serve around a campfire.

Moroccan orange salad

Serves 6

Ingredients
1 cup white sugar, plus
  2 tbsp extra
½ cup boiling water
6 large oranges
3 tbsp honey
A few fresh mint leaves, shredded
¼ cup unsalted pistachio halves

Method

1 Place 1 cup of sugar in a saucepan with 1 cup of water.

2 Set the pan over a low heat, stir until the sugar has dissolved, then raise the heat and bring to a boil without stirring.

3 Simmer until the sugar turns to caramel.

4 Remove from the heat and immediately pour in the boiling water, stirring well — take care because the caramel will spit.

5 Set the caramel syrup aside to cool.

6 Pare the zest from the oranges and cut it into thin strips.

7 Blanch the zest in a small saucepan of boiling water, then drain and refresh under cold running water.

8 Place the zest in a frying pan with the extra 2 tablespoons of sugar and a little water to cover.

9 Set the frying pan over a low heat, stir to dissolve the sugar, and cook until the zest has caramelized.

10 Remove the caramelized zest and place on a wire rack to harden.

11 Peel and slice the oranges, adding them to the caramel syrup.

12 Stir in the honey and mint to taste, then chill for several hours.

13 When almost ready to serve, toast the pistachio nuts in a dry frying pan until lightly browned; then set aside to cool.

14 Sprinkle the oranges with the pistachios and caramelized zest, then serve.

Dried apricots dipped in chocolate

Serves 12-14

Ingredients
7 oz dark bitter chocolate
2½ cups dried apricots

Method
1 Melt the chocolate in a bowl over a pan of simmering water.
2 Half-dip the apricots in the chocolate, transferring them to a tray lined with wax paper once they are coated.
3 Place in the fridge until set, then serve chilled with coffee.

Peanut brittle

Serves 10-12

Ingredients
Butter, for greasing
1¾ cups sugar
1 tbsp fresh lemon juice
2 cups raw peanuts, husks removed
⅓ cup sesame seeds (optional)

Method
1 Cover a baking tray with kitchen foil and lightly grease with butter.
2 Put the sugar in a saucepan with 3 tablespoons of water and place over a low heat, stirring constantly until the sugar turns to caramel.
3 Remove from the heat and carefully stir in the lemon juice.
4 Immediately add the peanuts and sesame seeds, if using.
5 Mix well and spoon the mixture onto the foil-lined tray.
6 Press the mixture flat using a palette knife and allow to set.
7 Break the peanut brittle into small pieces before serving.

Peanut brittle is best eaten on the day of making.

Chocolate-coated coffee beans

Serves 8

Ingredients
7 oz dark chocolate
2 oz espresso beans

Method
1 Melt the chocolate in a bowl over a pan of simmering water.
2 Stir in the espresso beans and mix until they are all coated in chocolate.
3 Spoon the mixture onto a tray lined with wax paper.
4 Place in the refrigerator to set.
5 Before serving, remove from the fridge and break into large pieces.

Don Pedro

Serves 4

Ingredients
8 shots Kahluha or whisky
8 scoops vanilla ice cream
1½ cups cream

Special equipment
Food processor

Method
1 Pour double shots of Kahluha or whisky into each serving glass.
2 Place the ice cream and cream in a food processor and quickly liquidize.
3 Carefully pour the ice cream mixture over the alcohol so that it floats, and serve the Don Pedros immediately.

Instead of pouring the ice cream mixture over the alcohol, you can liquidize them together to make a smooth and creamy after-dinner cocktail.

Index

Page numbers in italics refer to the photographs.

Resources

Safari lodges and camps

African Horseback Safaris
Okavango Delta
Macatoo Camp
P.O. Box 20538
Maun, Botswana
Tel/Fax: + 267 663 154
E-mail: sjhorses@info.bw

Ant Africa Safaris
P.O. Box 301
Vaalwater 0530
South Africa
Tel: + 27 83 287 2885
Fax: + 27 83 468 0237
E-mail: antafrica@waterberg.net

Makalali Game Reserve
P.O. Box 809
Hoedspruit 1380
South Africa
Tel: + 27 11 883 5786
Fax: + 27 11 883 4956
E-mail: makalali@aircon.co.za

Tongabezi
Private Bag 31
Livingstone, Zambia
Tel: + 260 3 323 235
Fax: + 260 3 323 224
E-mail: tonga@zammet.zm

Tswalu Desert Reserve Kalahari
P.O. Box 420
Kathu 8446
South Africa
Tel: + 27 537 819 311
Fax: + 27 537 819 316
E-mail: tswalures@kimberely.co.za

Uncharted Africa Safari Co
Jack's Camp
P.O. Box 173
Francistown
Botswana
Tel: + 267 212 277
Fax: + 267 213 458
E-mail: unchart@info.bw

Zimbabwe Sun Hotels, Resorts and
Lodges
P.O. Box 1671
Randburg, South Africa
Tel: + 27 11 886 2130
Fax: + 27 11 886 3432

Other resources

Colin Baber
Vaalwater Butchery
P.O. Box 302
Vaalwater 0503
South Africa
Tel/Fax: 27 147 553 611

Beith Digital
P.O. Box 76249
Wendywood 2144
Johannesburg
South Africa
Tel: 27 114 441 200
Fax: 27 114 442 859
Contact: Lisa Ransom

Speed Air (Pty) Ltd
Lanseria Airport
P.O. Box 310
Lanseria 1748
South Africa
Tel: 27 116 592 885
Fax: 27 116 591 748
Contact: Pikkie Grobbler

Acknowledgments

Our sincere thanks and gratitude go to all the people who made this book possible, particularly the people of Africa to whose joyous spirit this book is dedicated.

Special thanks are due to Liccy Dahl for being our Fairy Godmother. The book was Cathy O'Cleary's idea and we are very grateful for her generosity and vision at all stages. Lori-Ann Newman assisted with patience and vivacity and many of the recipes here are a result of her inspiration during our time together. Fred Stow helped with the text and was very involved with the logistics of planning our trip. We appreciate his endless support, encouragement and knowledge of the African bush.

Edward Van Lamp drove thousands of miles and steered us around creatures great and small. He had to be a real jack-of-all-trades, from mechanic to camera assistant. Charles and Nina Baber of Triple B Ranch graciously extended their hospitality and have become part of our extended family. Mercia Stow, Flick, and Zahn du Toit relayed messages and allowed us to use their offices. Pikkie Grobbler of Speed Air became a vital member of the team, bringing ingredients to us and film back to Johannesburg. Lisa Ransom of Beith Digital handled the film processing.

Tamsyn Hill organized much of the work from the London base-camp with great skill. Nicola Hill gave her time and proficiency in the publicity of the book, and Peter Dixon and Viv Yeo helped throughout.

We thank the staff of Conran Octopus and Jenni Muir and Leslie Harrington in particular for championing the project, also our designer Lawrence Morton for his inspired synthesis of the material.

At Tswalu, we would like to thank Jeanette Pulane, Emelda Jansen, Magdeline Shuping, Josephine Onewang, Reggie Assegaai, Ennie Tau and Monica Sechogela, Fritz Rabe, Stephan Jooste, Jaco Loots, Joanne Smart, Frances Markram, and Lucy Archer.

From African Horseback Safaris, thanks go to Sarah-Jane Gullick, John Southby, Beauty, Sarah and Senny. In addition Catherine Raephaely, Joe Charleson, Benson Mwendah, Nshai Lesupang, Baswazi & Derby from Uncharted Africa Safari Co. were a great help.

At Tongabezi, Julie Ruck Keene, Ben Parker, Clare Prideaux, Craig Higgins, George Kalaluka, Zuwi Nawa, Thomas Mwala and Rayness Himaanga generously provided assistance, so too Dave Bunyard and Darren Beatson of the Victoria Falls Hotel and Ant and Tessa Baber of Ant Africa Safaris. Much love and thanks also to all the makers, bakers and shakers of Makalali.